McDougal Littell
LITERATURE

InterActive
READER & WRITER

TEACHER'S GUIDE

LEVEL 1: *Strategic Reading Support*

LEVEL 2: *Critical Analysis*

Grade 9

 McDougal Littell

EVANSTON, ILLINOIS • BOSTON • DALLAS

ISBN 13: 978-0-618-90965-0   ISBN 10: 0-618-90965-6

Printed in the United States of America.

1 2 3 4 5 6 7 8 9–DOM–12 11 10 09 08

SENIOR PROGRAM CONSULTANTS

Janet Allen
Internationally-known Reading and Literacy Specialist

Arthur N. Applebee
Leading Professor, School of Education, University of Albany, State University of New York; Director of the Center on English Learning and Achievement

Jim Burke
Lecturer, Author, English Teacher, Burlingame, California

Douglas Carnine
Professor of Education, University of Oregon

Yvette Jackson
Executive Director, National Urban Alliance for Effective Education

Robert Jiménez
Professor of Language, Literacy, and Culture, Vanderbilt University

Judith A. Langer
Distinguished Professor, University of Albany, State University of New York; Director of the Center on English Learning and Achievement; Director of the Albany Institute for Research in Education

Robert J. Marzano
Senior Scholar, Mid-Continent Research for Education and Learning (McREL), Denver, Colorado

Donna M. Ogle
Professor of Reading and Language, National-Louis University, Chicago, Illinois; Past President, International Reading Association

Carol Booth Olson
Senior Lecturer, Department of Education, University of California, Irvine

Carol Ann Tomlinson
Professor of Educational Research, Foundations, and Policy, University of Virginia; Co-Director of the University's Institutes on Academic Diversity

ENGLISH LEARNER SPECIALISTS

Mary Lou McCloskey
Past President, TESOL; Director of Teacher Development and Curriculum Design for Educo, Atlanta, Georgia

Lydia Stack
Past President, TESOL; International ESL Consultant

CURRICULUM SPECIALIST

William L. McBride
Nationally-known Speaker, Educator, and Author

TABLE OF CONTENTS

What Is *The InterActive Reader & Writer?*

A book that helps all of your students develop stronger skills in

- **Reading**
- **Critical thinking**
- **Writing**
- **Test-taking**

The InterActive Reader & Writer is the "next generation" of *The InterActive Reader.* It has all the features teachers loved in the original:

- **Commonly-taught literature selections** from the *McDougal Littell Literature* core anthology, reproduced in their original form

- **A consumable format** that allows students to "interact" with the text, taking notes in the margins and responding to prompts

- **Side-column annotations** that foster reading comprehension and critical thinking

The InterActive Reader & Writer contains these new features:

- **Two different versions for students,** which can be used separately or together in the same classroom:

  —**Level 1: Strategic Reading Support** provides reading help for students reading at or below grade level.

  —**Level 2: Critical Analysis** develops and reinforces high-level critical thinking skills in students reading at or above grade level.

- **The same core literature at each level,** so all students have the opportunity to read and respond to the same great selections (However, annotations and activities differ in order to meet the needs of the particular group of students using it.)

- **Informational nonfiction texts at each level,** which engage students at their reading level

- **Integrated test preparation** that includes multiple-choice questions during and after reading, test tips, and practice responding to writing prompts.

Components

The InterActive Reader & Writer (in two versions)

These differentiated test practice readers pair the same anchor selections from the *McDougal Littell Literature* anthology units with different, leveled nonfiction readings.

The InterActive Reader & Writer with Strategic Reading Support (Level 1)

- For students reading at or below level
- Provides help in understanding literature
- High-interest nonfiction readings
- Multiple-choice items in state test formats
- Short- and extended-response writing

Strategic Reading Support side annotations help students use active reading strategies to monitor their comprehension and engage with the text.

The InterActive Reader & Writer for Critical Analysis (Level 2)

- For students reading at or above level/Pre-AP
- High-level analysis of literature
- More challenging nonfiction readings
- Multiple-choice items in state test formats
- Short- and extended-response writing

Critical Analysis side annotations challenge students to analyze what they read at a deeper level.

Teacher's Guide

A single Teacher's Guide provides lesson support for all selections in both levels. The Guide includes direct instruction, answer keys, support for English-language learners, writing rubrics, and guidelines for using both levels together in one classroom or using one level at a time.

Use for both levels

Special Features

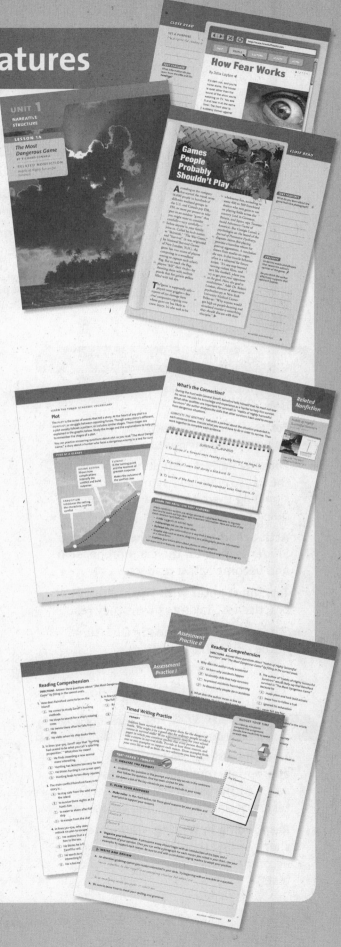

Strategies for Reading Nonfiction

- Each unit is a "cluster" made up of one **Anchor Selection** (common to Levels 1 and 2) and one or two pieces of **Related Nonfiction** (unique to each level).

- Nonfiction selections are appropriate for students' reading level (chosen for readability, concept load, vocabulary, and text sophistication).

- Each cluster of selections encourages students to synthesize information from different texts and find connections between ideas, presentations, and viewpoints.

- Nonfiction reading skills help students understand the features, organization, and characteristics of nonfiction text.

- Students learn about a variety of nonfiction formats.

Focus on Academic Vocabulary

- **Literary terms** for each anchor selection are introduced before students read, are used in side notes during reading, and are tested after reading.

- **Informational nonfiction terms** are taught before students begin reading the Related Nonfiction and are reinforced as students proceed through the text.

- **Additional Terms for Critical Analysis** are presented in the Level 2 book.

Assessment Practice

- The *InterActive Reader & Writer* offers a fresh, innovative way of helping students prepare for standardized tests. **Multiple-choice test questions** appear right next to the text they ask about. **Test Tips** demonstrate useful strategies students can use to answer them.

- One page of assessment practice at the end of each anchor selection (**Assessment Practice I**), and a second page of assessment practice after the Related Nonfiction (**Assessment Practice II**) give students the opportunity to practice the Test Tips they learned while reading.

- **A short written response** and **an extended timed writing assessment** are provided for each unit; included are step-by-step tips for planning and organizing written responses.

Two Levels—At a Glance

Reading the Anchor Selection

LEVEL 1

LEVEL 2

BEFORE READING—LEVELS 1 AND 2

- **The Big Question activity**
- **Assessment Goals** (Some goals are the same in both levels; others are different.)
- **Learn the Terms page** (One or two Additional Terms for Critical Analysis are presented in Level 2.)
- **Background paragraph**

DURING READING—LEVEL 1

- **Mark It Up**—Self-monitoring system is explained.
- **Focus**—Introduces each chunk of text; helps to set a purpose for reading
- **Pause & Reflect**—Students read until the Pause & Reflect symbol appears, signaling them to stop and answer the questions in the margins.
- **Active reading strategy notes**—Students monitor their comprehension and become active readers.
- **TestSmart notes with Tips**—Students practice test-taking skills as they read.
- Students return to the **Big Question** at the end of the selection.

DURING READING—LEVEL 2

- **Mark & Analyze**—Students read the anchor selection once all the way through, marking up the text in any way they like.
- **Second Read**—Students then read the text a second time, using the critical analysis annotations to deepen their understanding.
- **TestSmart notes with Tips**—Students practice test-taking skills as they read.
- Students return to the **Big Question** at the end of the selection.

AFTER READNG—LEVEL 1

- **Assessment Practice I**—Level 1-appropriate multiple-choice test items cover anchor selection, literary skills, test strategies taught, and vocabulary.
- **Responding in Writing**—Simulates short writing prompts that often accompany passages on standardized tests.

Certain test items are the same in both levels.

Writing prompt is the same in both levels.

AFTER READNG—LEVEL 2

- **Assessment Practice I**—Level 2-appropriate multiple-choice test items cover anchor selection, literary skills, test strategies taught, and vocabulary.
- **Responding in Writing**—Simulates short writing prompts that often accompany passages on standardized tests.

Continued on the next page . . .

Reading the Related Nonfiction

BEFORE READING—LEVEL 1

- **What's the Connection?**—Helps students relate the anchor selection to the Related Nonfiction found in the Level 1 book.
- **Learn the Skill**—Introduces the nonfiction skill for Level 1.
- Students set a purpose for reading the nonfiction selection(s) in Level 1.

▼

DURING READING—LEVEL 1

- Students apply the Level 1 nonfiction skill.
- **Specialized Vocabulary** notes explain words specific to certain careers or disciplines, jargon, technical terms, and so on.
- **TestSmarts with Tip**s give students the opportunity to further practice their test-taking skills.

▼

AFTER READING—LEVEL 1

- **Assessment Practice II**—Multiple-choice test items cover comprehension of the Related Nonfiction in Level 1; some questions require students to make connections between the various selections in the unit.
- **Timed Writing Response**—Extended-response writing prompt (e.g., persuasive essay, narrative, and so on). Step-by-step instructions help students plan and organize their responses and budget their time.

BEFORE READING—LEVEL 2

- **What's the Connection?**—Helps students relate the anchor selection to the Related Nonfiction found in the Level 2 book.
- **Learn the Skill**—Introduces the nonfiction skill for Level 2.
- Students set a purpose for reading the nonfiction selection(s) in Level 2.

▼

DURING READING—LEVEL 2

- Students apply the Level 2 nonfiction skill.
- **Specialized Vocabulary** notes explain words specific to certain careers or disciplines, jargon, technical terms, and so on.
- **TestSmarts with Tips** give students the opportunity to further practice their test-taking skills.

▼

AFTER READING—LEVEL 2

- **Assessment Practice II**—Multiple-choice test items cover comprehension of the Related Nonfiction in Level 2; some questions require students to synthesize information from all of the selections in the unit.
- **Timed Writing Response**—Extended-response writing prompt (e.g., persuasive essay, narrative, and so on). Step-by-step instructions help students plan and organize their responses and budget their time.

Writing prompt is the same in both levels, but the Test-Taker's Toolkit differs.

Despite the differences in the two levels, the pagination matches in both books. This makes it easy to use Levels 1 and 2 together in the same classroom.

Skills and Strategies for Reading and Thinking

The InterActive Reader & Writer helps all students become better strategic readers and more effective critical thinkers.

ALL STUDENTS

All students are encouraged to think critically by responding to questions that encourage them to:

- **Analyze**
- **Interpret**
- **Make Inferences**
- **Draw Conclusions**
- **Evaluate**
- **Make Judgments**

STRATEGIC READING SUPPORT (Level 1) focuses on active reading strategies. These are the strategies students are encouraged to use most often:

- **Preview**
- **Predict**
- **Visualize**
- **Clarify**
- **Connect**
- **Monitor**
- **Question**
- **Summarize**

CRITICAL ANALYSIS (Level 2) encourages students to think more deeply and critically about the selections they read. In addition to skills listed above and to the left, here are some of the more difficult critical thinking skills students will encounter at this level:

- **Compare/Contrast**
- **Classify**
- **Synthesize**
- **Make Generalizations**
- **Examine Perspectives**

Ways to Use *The InterActive Reader & Writer*

- ## In Conjunction with *McDougal Littell Literature*

  You may use *The InterActive Reader & Writer* as a differentiated, test-prep alternative to studying select works of literature. If *The InterActive Reader & Writer* is being used in conjunction with *McDougal Littell Literature,* you may wish to begin the prereading activities, such as the *Big Question* and *Learn the Terms,* in class; the main anthology can then be left at school while students carry home their smaller readers.

- ## After-School Program

  The InterActive Reader & Writer is appropriate for use in an after-school setting as a stand-alone test prep or reading comprehension program.

- ## Summer School or Summer Reading Program

  The InterActive Reader & Writer may be used as part of a summer academic enrichment program to sharpen students' reading and critical thinking skills and prepare them for the upcoming year.

- ## One-on-One or Small-Group Literacy Coaching

  Students reading below grade level may benefit from using *The InterActive Reader & Writer* with a literacy coach to develop reading comprehension skills and active reading strategies.

Suggested Reading Options

The InterActive Reader & Writer allows you to choose from a number of different reading options.

Independent Reading

Students can read independently, using the questions in the margins of their books for guidance and focus. Though this option is especially appropriate for students using Level 2, all students should have some opportunities to read independently.

Partner/Group Reading*

Students can read in pairs or small groups, pausing to discuss questions, write answers, and compare notations and highlighted passages.

Teacher Modeling*

This is especially appropriate for Level 1. Read aloud the first part of a selection, discuss key events or concepts that are important for comprehension, and then have students continue reading on their own. For particularly challenging selections, reading aloud can continue farther into the selection.

Oral Reading*

Students take turns reading portions of the text. This option works well for speeches, interviews, or stories and articles that contain dialogue. This option is also particularly useful for students using Level 1.

Audio Library*

Recordings of literature selections in *The InterActive Reader & Writer* are provided as part of the McDougal Littell Literature core program. You may find it useful to have students read along with these recordings.

Options marked with an asterisk (*) are especially effective with English Language Learners.

How Does *The InterActive Reader & Writer* Meet the Goals of Differentiation?

"[Differentiation] is simply a process of setting class goals, monitoring students' progress toward those goals, and teaching flexibly to help students progress toward and beyond those goals."

—Carol Ann Tomlinson, Ed.D., University of Virginia

Planning for Differentiation	The InterActive Reader & Writer
1 Begin at the end Decide what you want students to know, understand, and be able to do at the end of a specific lesson or unit. These essential goals should be the same for all students.	Assessment goals are established at the beginning of each unit.
2 Differentiate content, process, and product Adjust how students work, how sophisticated the task is, how difficult the reading material is, and what students are asked to produce.	*The InterActive Reader & Writer* offers leveled support within the same basic lesson framework.
3 Integrate ongoing assessment Monitor whether students are grasping concepts and mastering skills, or whether they need more instruction and support.	Assessment practice is integrated into every part of *The InterActive Reader & Writer,* allowing you to monitor students' progress throughout the unit.

How Do You Decide Which Version Is Appropriate?

There are many ways of assessing students' reading proficiency. These include formal, informal, and anecdotal measurements.

- Administer one or more of the **Diagnostic Assessments** at the back of this Teacher's Guide. These tools will help you decide which book each student should use.
- Observe students' habits and behaviors to help you determine their confidence with reading and writing and their general reading proficiency levels.

Students Who Struggle with Reading May...

- Regularly need additional time to complete reading assignments in class
- Avoid reading and/or writing
- Lack general and/or academic vocabulary
- Have difficulty attending to directions, conversations, tasks
- Appear to lack traits of skilled readers (surveying text, using graphics to support understanding, looking for context clues)
- Have difficulty summarizing or synthesizing text
- Move their lips as they read, or consistently follow text with a hand
- Pretend to read
- Frequently substitute one word for another when reading aloud

Students Who Are Proficient Readers May...

- Consistently finish reading and written work faster than most of the class
- Ask questions or make comments that go well beyond the simple sense of the text
- Give evidence of using traits of skilled readers
- Summarize or synthesize text readily and accurately
- Demonstrate content knowledge, background knowledge, and academic vocabulary
- Grasp key ideas quickly
- Make connections among ideas readily
- Read books for pleasure
- Respond positively to advanced-level or open-ended tasks because they provide challenge

Staying Flexible

If you have assigned a student to a version of *The InterActive Reader & Writer* that is clearly too challenging or too easy, you can easily move that student to the other version. Monitoring students' progress will help you remain flexible.

LESSON PLANS

The Most Dangerous Game
by Richard Connell

SUMMARY:

In this harrowing tale, hunter Sanger Rainsford becomes stranded on a remote island where he seeks help at the château of General Zaroff. Zaroff, also a hunter, seems cultured at first but then forces Rainsford to become his quarry in a hunt to the death. Zaroff seems destined to win, but Rainsford outwits Zaroff and kills him.

RELATED NONFICTION:

LEVEL 1

MAGAZINE ARTICLE: "Habits of Highly Successful Survivors"
This article examines the qualities and behaviors that survivors of dangerous situations share. (*Readability*: Average)

LEVEL 2

ONLINE ARTICLE: "How Fear Works"
This online article explores the function of the human brain in its response to fear. (*Readability*: Challenging)

MAGAZINE ARTICLE: "Games People Probably Shouldn't Play"
Should people take part in survival games in which players simulate killing one another? This magazine article ponders the question. (*Readability*: Average)

FOCUS AND MOTIVATE *p. 3*

FOR ALL STUDENTS

EXPLORE THE BIG QUESTION: *"What does it take to be a SURVIVOR?"*
Discuss the question with students, encouraging them to think about both mental and physical survival skills needed in an emergency. Then have them complete the **List It** activity and discuss their responses with a partner.

INTRODUCE THE LESSON Tell students that in this group of selections, they will explore how different people respond to frightening experiences. Then call their attention to the Assessment Goals at the bottom of the page.

ASSESSMENT GOALS

LEVEL 1

- analyze plot in a work of fiction
- use active reading strategies to comprehend text
- use text features to better understand nonfiction
- analyze a writing prompt and plan a persuasive essay

LEVEL 2

- analyze plot in a work of fiction
- apply critical thinking skills to analyze text
- use text features to navigate nonfiction
- analyze a writing prompt and plan a persuasive essay

LEVEL 1

To enhance students' understanding of the five stages of a plot, choose a familiar story, folk tale, or movie, and ask students to identify which plot points match each stage. Here is an example of how the first two plot stages could be tied to the story of Cinderella:

EXPOSITION: We meet Cinderella, her stepmother, and stepsisters. They live in a kingdom, several centuries ago.

RISING ACTION (INCLUDING CONFLICT): We learn that the stepmother favors her own daughters and treats Cinderella like a slave. The prince of the kingdom invites all the single women to a ball from which he will choose a bride. The stepmother forbids Cinderella to go.

LEVEL 2

If helpful, review the definitions of **plot** and **conflict.** You may wish to include these additional points:

FOR PLOT
- A story may begin in the middle of the action, and then return to the events that lead up to that point.
- The sequence of events may be interrupted to tell about an event that happened in the past or may happen in the future.
- A story may include subplots, or smaller stories within the larger one.

FOR CONFLICT
- A story may contain several conflicts, but the main conflict drives the plot.
- A conflict can be external (between the characters and an outside force), or internal (inside the character's mind).

ADDITIONAL TERMS FOR CRITICAL ANALYSIS

To reinforce understanding of **foreshadowing** and **suspense,** ask students for examples from their favorite books and movies. Include these points in your discussion:

FORESHADOWING
- may be created through dialogue, a change in mood, or an unusual character or event
- is particularly common in tales of suspense and horror

SUSPENSE
- can be created when the reader knows something a character does not, or when a situation is set up and the outcome isn't clear
- often is tied to the main conflict of a story

ADDITIONAL RESOURCES
from McDougal Littell Literature

STUDENT'S EDITION
Literary Analysis Workshop, "Plot Stages and Conflict," p. 24
Additional selection questions, p. 75

STANDARDS LESSON FILE: LITERATURE
Lesson 5: Elements of Plot, p. 41
Lesson 6: Conflict and Suspense, p. 51
Lesson 8: Foreshadowing and Flash- back, p. 69

RESOURCE MANAGER
Selection Summary, p. 51
Additional Selection Questions, p. 47
Ideas for Extension, p. 48
Vocabulary Study, p. 57
Vocabulary Practice, p. 58
Reading Check, p. 60
Question Support, p. 61
Selection Test A, p. 65
Selection Test B/C, p. 67

BEST PRACTICES TOOLKIT
Analysis Frame: Plot, p. D28
Plot Diagram, p. D10

VOCABULARY IN CONTEXT Read aloud the context phrases below and show students how to use context clues to figure out meaning. Once students have offered their own suggestions, review the actual definitions.

SELECTION VOCABULARY

tangible *(adj.)*: capable of being touched or felt; having actual form and substance (line 50)

quarry *(n.)*: the object of a hunt; prey (line 130)

disarming *(adj.)*: removing or overcoming suspicion; inspiring confidence (line 162)

cultivated *(adj.)*: refined or cultured in manner (line 176)

amenity *(n.)*: something that adds to one's comfort or convenience (line 222)

condone *(v.)*: to forgive or overlook (line 343)

droll *(adj.)*: amusingly odd or comical (line 345)

scruple *(n.)*: a feeling of uneasiness that keeps a person from doing something (line 354)

solicitously *(adv.)*: in a manner expressing care or concern (line 429)

imperative *(adj.)*: absolutely necessary (line 532)

zealous *(adj.)*: intensely enthusiastic (line 537)

uncanny *(adj.)*: so remarkable as to seem supernatural (line 568)

CONTEXT PHRASES

1. real and **tangible**

2. the hunter's **quarry**

3. put at ease by his **disarming** smile

4. a charming, **cultivated** woman

5. a cruise ship offering every **amenity**

6. **condone** rather than condemn

7. a **droll**, self-mocking grin

8. felt no **scruples** about breaking traffic laws

9. asked **solicitously** about my health

10. recommended but not **imperative**

11. **zealous** support of the mayor's program

12. an **uncanny** coincidence

Make sure students are familiar with the following idioms that appear in this story.

- **tight place** (line 82): difficult situation
- **making headway** (line 135): progressing
- **go to pieces** (line 293): lose self-control
- **held his tongue in check** (line 394): kept quiet

- **give you my word** (line 491): promise
- **got a grip on himself** (line 520): taken control of his feelings
- **taking stock of** (line 520): judging

The Most Dangerous Game

CLOSE READ

If you are using this selection primarily for **test preparation,** direct students to preview the multiple choice questions on page 25 and the writing prompt on page 26 to help focus their reading. Explain that this is a technique they should use any time they take a reading test.

Monitor, page 6

Answer: No. Students should underline "They've no understanding" (line 22).

Analyze, page 6

Students might underline the following:
- The place has a reputation—a bad one. (line 31)
- Even cannibals wouldn't live in such a Godforsaken place. (line 33)
- This place has an evil name among seafaring men (lines 39–40)
- as if the air about us was actually poisonous (line 41)
- evil place can . . . broadcast vibrations of evil (lines 51–52)

Students should check the word *forbidding. Remediation Tip:* Make sure all students understand the meaning of the word *forbidding.* If students have checked another word, ask them to show support for their answer. When they are unable to show support, explain that from the descriptions in the text, the only answer that makes sense is *forbidding.*

✓TestSmart page 7

Answer: B, "He tries to catch. . . ." Students should underline lines 73–74: "He lunged for it . . . lost his balance."

Make Inferences, page 7

Gunshots are fired by people; those people may help to save him.

Pause & Reflect, page 8

1. *MAKE INFERENCES* He doesn't panic or wear himself out by trying to swim after the ship. He is calm in a crisis and conserves his strength. He uses good judgment to find the shore. He is strong enough to climb the cliffs.
2. *CLARIFY* Rainsford's main conflict so far has been to survive in the dangerous sea.

Visualize, page 9

Students might underline the following words and phrases:
- many lights (line 140)
- one enormous building (line 141)
- a lofty structure with pointed towers plunging upward into the gloom (lines 141–142)
- palatial château (line 143)
- set on a high bluff (lines 143–144)
- on three sides of it cliffs dived down (line 144)
- spiked iron gate. The stone steps (line 147)
- massive door with a leering gargoyle for a knocker (line 148)

Students should check *imposing* and *forbidding.*

Make Inferences, page 9

Answer: No. Students might underline evidence that the door knocker seems like it has never been used and the bearded man's behavior is extreme.

Monitor, page 10

Students might circle the following:
- cultivated voice (line 176)
- singularly handsome (line 182)
- bizarre quality about the general's face (lines 183–184)
- tall man past middle age (line 184)
- the face of a man used to giving orders, the face of an aristocrat (line 188)
- He is a Cossack. . . . So am I. (lines 195–196)

The impression students might have of General Zaroff is that he is a gracious yet mysterious host. He seems used to being in control of situations.

Pause & Reflect, page 11

1. *DRAW CONCLUSIONS* Students should write line numbers 180 and 213–215.
2. *MAKE INFERENCES* Possible responses:
   - The general is trying to learn more about Rainsford to make sure he is not dangerous.
   - The general is interested to see what the man he has read about—the celebrated hunter—is like.

Accept other reasonable inferences.

✓TestSmart page 12

Answer: A, passionate. *Remediation Tip:* If students choose the incorrect answer, make sure they substitute each of the answer options in the sentence in which *ardent* appears. They should see that only *passionate* makes sense.

Monitor, page 13

Students should underline lines 291–292: "Hunting was beginning to bore me!"

Predict, page 13

Accept any response the student is able to support.

Pause & Reflect, page 14

MAKE INFERENCES Students should underline line 330: "It must have courage . . . it must be able to reason." Students should infer that the general hunts humans. Only humans are able to reason.

Monitor, page 15

Students should underline the following: "Sometimes an angry god . . . sends them to me" (lines 367–368); "They indicate a channel . . . crush this nut" (lines 374–376)

Question, page 15

Students should underline the following: "They get plenty of good food and exercise. They get into splendid physical condition." (lines 385–386) *Possible response:* The visitors will be more of a challenge for Zaroff to hunt if they are strong and healthy.

Clarify, page 16

Students should underline lines 403–405: "If he does not wish to hunt . . . he has his own ideas of sport."

Compare, page 16

Students should complete the first sentence by saying that both men enjoy hunting. Students should complete the second sentence by explaining that Rainsford disagrees with Zaroff's ideas about hunting humans.

Pause & Reflect, page 17

EVALUATE The person being hunted gets food, a hunting knife, and a three-hour head start. *Possible response:* No, the game is not fair. The rules favor Zaroff.

✓**TestSmart** page 18

Answer: D, "The general believes they are both skilled enough. . . ." Students should underline lines 484–485: "Your brain against mine. . . . Outdoor chess!"

Pause & Reflect, page 19

1. *ANALYZE* Students should underline lines 517–519: "His whole idea at first . . . very like panic." The tactic is not good because it is a panicked response rather than a reasoned response. It would bring him straight to the sea and leave a clear path for Zaroff to follow.

2. *CLARIFY* Students should check the second box: "He knows that Zaroff is an excellent hunter. . . ." *Remediation Tip:* If students check the first box, explain that they chose Rainsford's first response, one that Rainsford realizes was ineffective. He then came up with his "fox trail" plan as a better way to throw off Zaroff.

Visualize, page 20

Students might underline the following:

- He made his way . . . and studied the ground. (lines 549–551)
- shook his head . . . as if he were puzzled (line 555)
- took from his case one of his black cigarettes (line 556)
- eyes . . . were traveling inch by inch up the tree (lines 558–559)
- smile spread over his brown face (line 561)

Connect, page 20

Students will probably say that they would be terrified and would need to make a better plan for the next day.

✓**TestSmart** **Vocabulary**, page 21

Answer: D, bandaged. *Remediation Tip:* If students struggle to find the correct answer, have them replace the word *dressed* with all of the answer choices to see which one makes the most sense.

Pause & Reflect, page 22

1. *MONITOR* Students should check the first and third boxes. If students can't remember the tactics, have them reread lines 588–643.

2. *ANALYZE* Students should underline line 641 in which Zaroff announces his plan to use his whole pack of dogs the next day. This intensifies the plot because Rainsford is in even more danger and must think of a very clever plan to stay alive.

Predict, page 23

Answers will vary. Students might circle Zaroff because he has the dogs and Ivan. They might circle Rainsford because he shows clever survival skills and is the "hero" of the story. Either way, students should provide clear reasoning for their choice.

Monitor, page 24

Zaroff is bothered that it will be difficult to replace Ivan (who is dead) and that Rainsford had escaped him. Students should underline lines 691–692.

Pause & Reflect, page 24

CLARIFY The conflict is resolved when Rainsford wins the fight against Zaroff. Students should underline the last sentence of the story, which makes it clear that Rainsford gets to sleep in the bed because he killed Zaroff.

Big Question page 24

Allow any well-supported answer. You may want to have students discuss their answers in small groups.

ASSESSMENT PRACTICE I: *p. 25*	
1. C	5. D
2. B	6. D
3. B	7. A
4. A	8. D

Point out to students that the test-taking strategies they learned as they read can be used with the following items:

- Item 1: cause and effect question (page 7)
- Items 2, 4, 5: specific lines from the text (page 18)
- Item 7: multiple-meaning words (page 21)
- Item 8: vocabulary from context (page 12)

The Most Dangerous Game

SECOND READ: CRITICAL ANALYSIS

If you are using this selection primarily for **test preparation,** direct students to preview the multiple choice questions on page 25 and the writing prompt on page 26 to help focus their reading. Explain that they can use this technique any time they take a reading test.

Analyze, page 5

Students might underline the following:

- Ship-Trap Island (line 4)
- suggestive name (line 5)
- curious dread of the place (line 5)
- the dank tropical night . . . upon the yacht (lines 7–9)
- a moonless, Caribbean night (line 12)

The name of the island foreshadows the way Zaroff traps people to hunt, and the description of sailors' "curious dread" foreshadows the horrific acts that take place on the island.

Draw Conclusions, page 6

Students might underline the following:

- The best sport in the world (line 17)
- Who cares how a jaguar feels? (line 20)
- The world is made up of two classes . . . you and I are hunters. (lines 26–27)

Rainsford probably does not hold these opinions at the end of the story. He becomes a "huntee" for the first time, which likely changes his feelings about hunting in general.

Evaluate, page 7

Students will likely conclude that the rising action begins when Rainsford falls off the ship. At that point, the initial problem has been presented, and the plot starts to build suspense.

However, it is also acceptable if students choose "when he finds out about the hunt," as long as they are able to support their opinion. These students might argue that Rainsford's initial conflict (surviving the sea) merely sets up the story and that meeting the other characters is part of the exposition. They may say that the complications really begin after Rainsford learns about the hunt.

Analyze, page 7

Students might underline the following:

- struggled up . . . cry out (line 77)
- Desperately he struck out (line 79)
- A certain cool-headedness . . . tight place. (lines 81–82)
- He wrestled . . . shouted with all his power. (lines 84–85)
- doggedly he swam . . . conserving his strength (lines 89–90)

Rainsford is also courageous and resourceful when he outwits Zaroff later in the story.

Classify, page 8

Students should check the first box: *man vs. nature.* Rainsford has struggled against the sea.

Analyze, page 8

Students might underline

- But what kind . . . forbidding a place? (lines 117–118)
- Some wounded thing . . . stained crimson. (lines 122–124)
- A twenty-two (line 127)
- It's clear that . . . a fight. (line 129)

Visualize, page 9

Students might underline

- there were many lights (line 140)
- one enormous building . . . pointed towers" (lines 141–142)
- palatial château (line (143)
- set on a high bluff (lines 143–144)
- spiked iron gate. The stone steps (line 147)
- massive door (line 148)

Students might circle

- Bleak darkness (line 137)
- the gloom (line 142)
- shadowy outlines (line 143)
- cliffs . . . in the shadows (line 144–145)
- leering gargoyle (line 148)
- air of unreality (line 149)

✓TestSmart page 10

Answer: C, "like all his race, . . ." Zaroff describes Cossacks as savages, and then he admits that he is a Cossack. Therefore, he considers himself to be a savage, which foreshadows his behavior later in the story when he hunts humans.

Interpret, page 11

Possible response: It is ironic because Zaroff gives the outward appearance of having a dignified and civilized life, but he is actually a cold-blooded killer.

Analyze, page 12

Students might underline the following sentences: "I live for danger, Mr. Rainsford." (line 255) and "Me he made a hunter." (line 267). These traits explain that Zaroff sees it as part of his nature to hunt humans.

Analyze, page 13

Connell builds suspense by allowing readers (and Rainsford) to slowly figure out what type of animal Zaroff hunts. Students might underline the following lines:

- Hunting was beginning to bore me! (lines 291–292)
- ceased to be . . . 'a sporting proposition' (lines 304–305)
- Instinct is no match for reason. (line 310)
- invent a new animal to hunt (line 316)

Make Inferences, page 14

The "ideal animal to hunt" is the human. Students should underline:

- it must be able to reason (line 330)
- there is one that can (line 332)
- what you speak of is murder (lines 337–338)

Compare, page 15

Both men divide the world into two camps. Zaroff describes the strong and the weak; Rainsford describes hunters and huntees. Both men believe that it is natural for the strong to hunt the weak.

Analyze, page 15
The contrast in Zaroff's mood adds suspense because it indicates that Rainsford may be in danger.

✓TestSmart page 15
Answer: A, poor quality. "Poor specimens" in line 391 provides students with the context to make the correct choice.

Analyze, page 16
Zaroff establishes himself as a difficult person to beat in future hunts, which adds to the tension in the rising action.

Make Judgments, page 16
No. Zaroff has not created a fair game. He has a gun, knows the island, and can use his dogs for tracking. He has an unfair advantage. Students might underline the following:
• armed only with a pistol (lines 397–398)
• If he does not wish to hunt . . . ideas of sport. (lines 403–405)
• I eventually had to use the dogs (lines 412–413)

Analyze, page 17
Students might underline the following:
• Once he thought . . . his room. (lines 439–440)
• He sought . . . it would not open. (lines 440–441)
• there, weaving in and out . . . green eyes (lines 444–447)
• the faint report of a pistol (lines 449–450)

✓TestSmart page 18
Answer: D, "The general believes they are both skilled enough . . . ." Students should underline lines 484–485: "Your brain against mine. . . . Outdoor chess!"

Interpret, page 19
Connell omits whatever happens between the time Rainsford receives supplies from Ivan and two hours later, after he'd fought through the bush. The author may have omitted these details to focus on the action and suspense of the early part of the hunt.

Draw Conclusions, page 20
Zaroff considers himself a skilled hunter and enjoys the challenge of the hunt, so he wants it to continue. He may also enjoy the idea that his actions terrify Rainsford.

✓TestSmart Vocabulary, page 21
Answer: B, advanced. Read the test-taking tip, and remind students to reread the sentence in which *pressed* was used before choosing their answer.

Connect, page 22
Students should think of a time in their own lives when their fear made a moment seem endless. Possible responses: waiting outside the principal's office; hearing a strange noise in the middle of the night.

Analyze, page 23
Students should underline the last sentence in the paragraph: "Rainsford knew now how an animal at bay feels." (lines 665–666). Rainsford's attitude has changed because he now understands what it's like to be hunted. At the beginning of the story, he had no sympathy for the animals he hunted.

✓TestSmart page 23
Answer: C, "the falling action" Read the test-taking tip, and ask students to read lines 677–682. If students can recognize this paragraph as the story's climax, or its highest point of action, then they should be able to conclude that the falling action starts in line 683.

Evaluate, page 24
The author has not described the final fight between Zaroff and Rainsford. The reader doesn't have any clues to figure out who gains the upper hand in the fight, so the surprise is held until the end of the story's final sentence.

Big Question page 24
Allow any well-supported answer. You may wish to discuss this question in a large group and keep a tally of students' responses.

ASSESSMENT PRACTICE I: *p. 25*	
1. A	5. B
2. C	6. D
3. B	7. A
4. D	8. D

Point out to students that the test-taking strategies they learned as they read can be used with the following items:
• Item 2: recognize foreshadowing (page 10)
• Items 3, 4: quotations from the text (page 18)
• Item 6: identify stages of plot (page 23)
• Item 7: multiple-meaning words (page 21)
• Item 8: vocabulary from context (page 15)

SHORT RESPONSE: PLOT SUMMARY Use this writing activity to determine whether students understand the elements of a plot and the structure of a story. Take them through the following steps:

- Have students analyze the prompt. They should notice that they are being asked to write one or two paragraphs.
- Have them complete the story map. Point out that if it is done correctly, it will contain most of the content they need to describe how the plot continues. Make sure they know, however, that they still have to add additional detail.
- Remind students to be creative. Once they have completed their work, you may wish to duplicate the models shown here on a copy master or transparency. Have students compare the ideas in the models with their own extended plots.

TEST-TAKER'S TOOLKIT

SETTING

> **WHERE:** *Ship-Trap Island*
>
> **WHEN:** *the morning after Rainsford kills Zaroff*

CHARACTERS: *Rainsford; the sailors in the cellar*

CONFLICT: *Rainsford and the remaining sailors trapped in the cellar need to get off the island*

HOW THE CONFLICT IS RESOLVED: *They discover Zaroff's sailboat and sail to the mainland.*

SAMPLE SUMMARY

Rainsford awoke from a deep sleep in Zaroff's comfortable bed. The memories from the past few days came flooding back immediately. Rainsford felt a tremendous sense of relief that he had killed Zaroff, but he realized he had a new problem: he had to find a way off the island.

He went to the kitchen for some food and heard noises that startled him. At first he thought it was Zaroff's dogs, but they were gated up in the courtyard. Then he remembered that Zaroff had intended to hunt sailors trapped in the cellar. He rushed down the stairs and released the nine remaining sailors. Together, Rainsford and the sailors came up with a plan to get off the island. They knew Zaroff had a boat. After much searching, they finally discovered it on a remote part of the island. They sailed off that evening, leaving the dogs and horrible memories behind.

SETTING A PURPOSE Complete the prereading activity on page 27 and review the teaching options below. Then share with your students what their goals will be, and use these goals to set a purpose for reading. Once students are clear on that purpose, have them write a purpose statement at the top of page 28.

TEST PREPARATION Direct students to read the multiple-choice questions on page 32, as well as the writing prompt on page 33, to help them focus their reading.

LEVEL 1

• Habits of Highly Successful Survivors

FOCUS SKILL: USE TEXT FEATURES

ACTIVITY: COMPLETE THE SENTENCE

The day before assigning the related readings, introduce the survival planning questions for students to think about outside of class. The following day, have students work in pairs to complete each sentence.

OPTIONS FOR TEACHING

SKILL INSTRUCTION Use "Learn the Skill" at the bottom of page 27 and page R2 in the Nonfiction Skills Handbook to review the focus skill of using text features.

> **ADDITIONAL RESOURCES:**
> **STANDARDS LESSON FILE:** READING AND INFORMATIONAL TEXTS: Text Features, page 171

JIGSAW LEARNING Divide the class into small groups, each responsible for learning and then sharing information about one of the following topics:
- Outdoor survival skills
- Psychological and physical responses to danger

If you are using Level 2 in the same classroom, add the "How Fear Works" article to the list of resources for the second topic. Add a third topic about whether people should take part in activities that simulate danger and use "Games People Probably Shouldn't Play" as a resource.

INVESTIGATION Have students investigate famous natural disasters and look for common experiences among those who survived.

LEVEL 2

• How Fear Works

• Games People Probably Shouldn't Play

FOCUS SKILL: ANALYZE TEXT FEATURES

ACTIVITY: CONDUCT A SURVEY

Have students complete the activity on page 27 about their physical reactions to a dangerous situation and an unnerving situation. Students should then evaluate the responses and reach a conclusion about whether people react differently to different types of fear.

OPTIONS FOR TEACHING

SKILL INSTRUCTION Use "Learn the Skill" at the bottom of page 27 and page R2 in the Nonfiction Skills Handbook to review the focus skill of analyzing text features.

> **ADDITIONAL RESOURCES:**
> **STANDARDS LESSON FILE:** READING AND INFORMATIONAL TEXTS: Text Features, page 171

JIGSAW LEARNING Divide the class into small groups, each responsible for learning and then sharing information about one of the following topics:
- Psychological and physical responses to danger
- Whether people should take part in activities that simulate danger

If you are using Level 1 in the same classroom, add "Habits of Highly Successful Survivors" to the list of resources for the first topic.

DEBATE Use "Games People Probably Shouldn't Play" as the basis for a debate about simulated war games. Encourage students to find additional information supporting their opinion about whether such games are harmless or harmful.

Habits of Highly Successful Survivors

Text Features, page 28
Students should respond that the article will be about the behaviors that survivors of dangerous situations share.

Text Features, page 29
Students should check the third box: THINK, ANALYZE, PLAN.

Specialized Vocabulary, page 29
Possible answer: thought. *Remediation Tip:* Have students replace *cognition* with their answer and see if the sentence still makes sense.

✓TestSmart page 30
Answer: C, Take Action. Remind students to notice the headings as they reread text.

Clarify, page 30
Students should underline the following:
- helps keep motivation high (line 76)
- prevents a lethal plunge into despair (line 76)
- provides relief from . . . situation (lines 77–78)

Make Judgments, page 31
Students should provide clear reasons why they admire the person they choose.

ASSESSMENT PRACTICE II: *p. 32*	
1. B	5. A
2. C	6. B
3. A	7. C
4. D	8. D

How Fear Works

Text Features, page 28
Most students will say the title and headings suggest that they will learn about what fear is, how the brain is involved in responding to fear, and what the fight-or-flight response is. Students should circle the heading "What Is Fear?"

Specialized Vocabulary, page 29
Students should underline "Some of these communications . . . run its course." (lines 26–29) The context makes it clear that *autonomic* means the opposite of *conscious.* Possible response: "not conscious; involuntary."

Text Features, page 29
Students should circle the sensory cortex at the top of the diagram.

✓TestSmart page 29
Answer: C, "hypothalamus"; Students should underline "activates a response" in the question and "activates 'fight-or-flight' response" in line 42.

Specialized Vocabulary, page 30
Students should underline the following:
- overall effect . . . very alert (lines 52–53)
- sends out impulses . . . into the bloodstream (lines 54–56)
- cause several changes . . . blood pressure (lines 57–58)

Text Features, page 30
The bulleted list describes the body's response to the hormones released during a threat.

Games People Probably Shouldn't Play

Text Features, page 31
The photo makes it clear that the game involves some type of gun and a splattered substance.

Evaluate, page 31
Students might underline "consider carefully—very carefully—before anyone in your family joins in" (lines 8–11) and "supposedly safe" (line 24). Students must decide if the author effectively supports his or her opinion by noting the amount and the type of evidence the author provides, such as quotations from psychologists and reports of eye damage.

ASSESSMENT PRACTICE II: *p. 32*	
1. C	5. A
2. B	6. C
3. B	7. B
4. D	8. C

LEVEL 1

Guide students through the steps described below under Guided Instruction. You may also wish to go over the rubric on the next page. (Consider modifying the rubric for these students, focusing only on Ideas, Organization, and Conventions.) Give students the entire 45 minutes to draft and review their responses. Point out, however, that in an actual timed writing situation, all steps of the writing process must be completed within the given time frame.

LEVEL 2

Share with students the rubric on the next page. Direct them to complete the entire writing process independently, within the actual 45-minute time frame they have been given.

GUIDED INSTRUCTION

ANALYZE THE PROMPT If necessary, lead students through the two-step analysis process on page 33. Explain that low scores are often the result of the writer missing a critical piece of the directions. The marked prompt should look like this:

> Soldiers learn survival skills to prepare them for the dangers of battle. Why might it be a good idea for ordinary people to take a course in survival skills? Write a persuasive essay for your school paper in which you convince readers that every person should take a course in survival skills. Provide at least three reasons, and one or two examples to support each reason. Draw examples from your own life as well as from the two selections you have read.

- You may want to point out that the last sentence indicates that students should draw examples from their personal experience. This means students can use the pronoun *I*.

- *Academic Vocabulary*: Students are asked to write a **persuasive essay.** Explain that this means that they need to convince their readers to adopt their opinion. Counsel them to choose the most persuasive examples to support their position.

Remind students that most or all of the circled words and phrases should be in the list of key elements they jot down, and all must all be addressed in their response if they want to achieve the highest score on the test.

PLAN YOUR RESPONSE

- Review with students the steps of a timed writing assignment. For a prompt like this, which requires them to find evidence, remind them to budget enough time to find support in the selections. (They should probably spend no more than 10–15 minutes identifying their examples.)

- Students should jot down notes and examples for each label in the chart. Point out, however, that in a real testing situation they would have had to supply these labels. Show them how the key words from the prompt suggested what those labels should be.

WRITE AND REVIEW Encourage students to try several different openings for their essay (using peer feedback to choose the best if time allows). When they have completed their draft, allow peers to comment on how well the students have met the requirements of the prompt.

RUBRIC FOR TIMED WRITING*

Key Traits	3 (Strong)	2 (Average)	1 (Weak)
IDEAS	• The thesis statement is focused, and clearly identifies the issue and the writer's position. • Relevant details and examples support each key idea. • The writer clearly explains how the examples are relevant to the position.	• The thesis statement is too broad or too narrow but loosely identifies the issue and the writer's position. • Most key ideas are supported by details and examples. • The writer usually explains how the examples are relevant to the position.	• The thesis statement is unclear or missing. • Details and examples are not relevant or are too scarce to support the key ideas. • The writer does not explain how the examples are relevant to the position.
ORGANIZATION	• The introduction clearly presents the issue and draws the reader in. • The conclusion summarizes the ideas and makes a call to action or call to agreement. • Transitional words and phrases clearly show how ideas connect. • The organization is logical and follows a consistent pattern.	• The introduction presents the issue, but it does not draw the reader in. • The conclusion summarizes the ideas but only restates what has been said. • Most of the transitions work, but a few more are needed. • The organization shows some logic but is inconsistent.	• The introduction does not clearly set up what the essay is about. • The essay lacks an identifiable conclusion. • The writer uses few, if any, transitional words. • The organization feels random or disjointed; the reader often feels lost or confused.
VOICE	• The tone and voice are appropriate for the purpose and audience. • The writing reflects active engagement with the topic.	• The tone and voice are acceptable for the purpose and audience but not strongly individual or direct. • The writing lacks consistent engagement with the topic.	• The voice lacks individuality and is not concerned with or not matched to the audience. • The writing reflects no engagement with the topic.
WORD CHOICE	• Words and phrases are used to persuade effectively. • Logic is sound, and appeals to emotion are appropriate.	• Familiar words and phrases communicate but rarely persuade the reader. • Some errors in logic and inappropriate appeals to emotion are present.	• Limited vocabulary and/or frequent misuse of parts of speech impair understanding. • Frequent errors in logic and inappropriate appeals to emotion distract the reader.
SENTENCE FLUENCY	• Sentences vary in length and structure. • Sentence beginnings are varied.	• Sentences do not significantly vary in structure, and some fragments and run-on sentences are present. • Sentence beginnings are mostly the same.	• Repetitive sentence structure, fragments, and run-on sentences make the writing difficult to follow. • Most or all sentences begin the same way.
CONVENTIONS	• Spelling, capitalization, and punctuation are generally correct. • Grammar and usage are correct. • Paragraphing tends to be correct and reinforces the organization.	• Spelling, capitalization, and punctuation are sometimes uneven. • Grammar and usage do not distort meaning but are not always correct. • Paragraphing is attempted but is not always sound.	• Spelling, capitalization, and punctuation are frequently incorrect. • Grammar and usage mistakes are frequent and distort meaning. • Paragraphing is missing, irregular, or too frequent.

*Use the Persuasive Essay Rubric on the WriteSmart CD if you wish to further modify this chart.

The Rights to the Streets of Memphis

by Richard Wright

SUMMARY:

In this excerpt from his autobiography, *Black Boy*, Richard Wright recalls a turning point in his childhood. Sent to buy groceries, Wright is twice robbed by a gang of boys. His mother gives him a heavy stick and orders him to stand up for himself. Though terrified, Wright fends off the gang and returns home with the groceries—and a new sense of self-respect.

RELATED NONFICTION:

LEVEL 1

BROCHURE: "Bullying Myths and Facts"
This brochure defines bullying and debunks several myths. (*Readability*: Average)

ONLINE ARTICLE: "What Can You Do If Someone Is Bullying You?"
This online article offers tips for dealing with bullies. (*Readability*: Easy)

LEVEL 2

BOOK REVIEW: "Books of the Times: *Black Boy*"
A book reviewer in 1945 points out positive and negative aspects of Richard Wright's *Black Boy*. (*Readability*: Challenging)

FOCUS AND MOTIVATE *p. 35*

FOR ALL STUDENTS

EXPLORE THE BIG QUESTION: *"What is worth FIGHTING FOR?"*
Discuss the question with students, prompting them to consider both individual issues and group concerns as part of the discussion. Then have them complete the **List It** activity, and have each group's spokesperson present their ideas to the class. Ask students to consider whether they wish to add to their lists after reading the selection.

INTRODUCE THE LESSON Tell students that in these selections, they will examine the different ways in which people stand up for themselves. Students in Level 1 will read two short articles about the nature of bullying and how to deal with bullies. Students in Level 2 will read one man's reaction to *Black Boy*, the book from which "The Rights to the Streets of Memphis" was taken. Then call their attention to the Assessment Goals at the bottom of the page.

ASSESSMENT GOALS

LEVEL 1

- identify conflict in an autobiography
- use active reading strategies to comprehend text
- identify an author's purpose and audience while reading nonfiction text
- analyze a writing prompt and plan an expository essay

LEVEL 2

- analyze conflict in an autobiography
- apply critical thinking skills to analyze text
- identify an author's purpose and audience while reading nonfiction text
- analyze a writing prompt and plan an expository essay

LEVEL 1

To help students recognize the different types of conflict, choose a familiar comic book hero who faces both an internal and an external conflict, and ask students to identify each. An example follows of how the character Peter Parker in the comic series *Spider-Man* is faced with both internal and external conflict.

INTERNAL CONFLICT: Peter feels responsible for his uncle's death when a thief Peter allowed to get away later kills his uncle. His regret and self-doubt drive him to stop crime, but he still longs to lead a normal life.

EXTERNAL CONFLICT: In each comic book, Peter faces a villain: Green Goblin, Doc Ock, Venom, Sandman, Rose, and others. The villains are trying to commit a dastardly crime, and Peter (as Spider-Man) must stop them.

LEVEL 2

If helpful, review the definitions of internal conflict and external conflict. You may wish to include these additional points:

FOR INTERNAL CONFLICT

- Internal conflict may be discussed by the narrator or discovered by the reader through the character's actions.
- The end result of internal conflict is usually a change for the character.
- Internal conflict may drive or exacerbate external conflict.

FOR EXTERNAL CONFLICT

- External conflict usually involves the antagonist.
- External conflict is not limited to conflict between people. The conflict can be between the character and a single antagonist, a group of people, or the forces of nature.
- External conflict may drive or exacerbate internal conflict.

ADDITIONAL TERMS FOR CRITICAL ANALYSIS

To reinforce understanding of **dialogue,** have a pair of students read aloud a section of dialogue between Wright and his mother (for example, lines 14–36). They should leave out any words that do not appear in quotation marks. In your discussion, point out that

- realistic dialogue is natural-sounding
- this dialogue is short and clipped, as a real-life exchange would be
- when the narrator is speaking in dialogue, his voice is different from his speech in the story

To reinforce understanding of **protagonists** and **antagonists,** invite students to list protagonists and antagonists from their favorite fairy tales or children's stories. Include these points in your discussion:

- Sometimes a story has more than one protagonist (as in "Hansel and Gretel").
- The protagonist, while usually the hero, is not always perfect.

ADDITIONAL RESOURCES
from **McDougal Littell Literature**

STUDENT'S EDITION
Literary Analysis Workshop, "Plot and Conflict," p. 24
Additional selection questions, p. 117

STANDARDS LESSON FILE: LITERATURE
Lesson 5: Elements of Plot, p. 41
Lesson 6: Conflict and Suspense, p. 51
Lesson 43: Dialogue and Dialect, p 409

RESOURCE MANAGER
Selection Summary, p. 139
Additional Selection Questions, p. 135
Ideas for Extension, p. 136
Vocabulary Study, p. 145
Vocabulary Practice, p. 146
Reading Check, p. 148
Question Support, p. 149
Selection Test A, p. 153
Selection Test B/C, p. 155

BEST PRACTICES TOOLKIT
Analysis Frame: Plot, p. D28
Plot Diagram, pp. D10, D55
Characters and Dialogue, pp. D8, D53

VOCABULARY IN CONTEXT Read aloud the context phrases below and show students how to use context clues to figure out meaning. Once students have offered their own suggestions, review the actual definitions.

SELECTION VOCABULARY

clamor *(n.)*: a noisy outburst; outcry (line 9)
dispirited *(adj.)*: dejected (line 58)
retaliate *(v.)*: to pay back an injury in kind (line 131)
flay *(v.)*: to whip or lash (line 133)
stark *(adj.)*: complete or utter; extreme (line 133)

CONTEXT PHRASES

1. **clamor** of children arriving at the playground

2. feeling discouraged and **dispirited**

3. wanting to **retaliate** for an offense

4. **flay** the ground wildly

5. **stark** difference between the brothers

Make sure students are familiar with the following terms and references that appear in this story.

Idioms Review and discuss the following expressions with students.

- **the days slid past** (line 53): time passed
- **yanked me to my feet** (line 90): pulled me to a standing position
- **froze in my tracks** (line 96): stopped suddenly and did not move
- **let up** (line 131): stopped
- **to lay them low, to knock them cold** (line 132): to hit them so hard that they couldn't move
- **egging them on** (line 137): urging them to do something
- **tore out** (line 139): ran away quickly

Cultural References Guide students to use context clues to better understand the following reference.

- **flat** (line 57): small apartment

The Rights to the Streets of Memphis

CLOSE READ

If you are using this selection primarily for **test preparation**, direct students to preview the multiple choice questions on page 42 and the writing prompt on page 43 to help focus their reading. Explain that this technique may be used any time they take a reading test.

Clarify, page 38

Students should check the first box: *external*. They might explain that the narrator is hungry, but there is no food. Students may circle "I want to eat" (line 24), "there's nothing to eat" (line 27). Point out that while hunger is an internal sensation, it is not an internal conflict; the reason for the hunger is coming from outside the narrator's body.

✓TestSmart page 38

Answer: A, Students should underline "I had been glad that he was not there" (lines 42–43); "deep biological bitterness" (lines 54–55).

Pause & Reflect, page 39

DRAW CONCLUSIONS Possible response: Wright is in conflict with his family's situation. Though he is still a child, he has to take care of himself because his father has abandoned the family. Students may underline "half frightened" (line 64) and "vague dread" (line 66). *Remediation Tip:* If students identify hunger as Wright's conflict, suggest that they reread lines 56–68. Ask them to find support for their answer in this paragraph. When they are unable to do so, point out that the narrator's hunger has been somewhat alleviated by the loaf of bread and the tea his mother has provided.

Evaluate & Connect, page 40

Students' responses will vary. Some may say that Wright's mother is being unnecessarily tough on him, while others will point out that she's teaching him a necessary lesson about standing up for himself.

✓TestSmart Vocabulary, page 40

Answer: B, unfriendly. Students may underline "gangs were after me," (lines 118–119) and "being beaten" (line 119).

Pause & Reflect, page 41

PREDICT Possible response: The narrator will be stronger, tougher, and less afraid because he has faced his fear by confronting the gang. Students may underline
- every ounce of my strength (line 134)
- taunting them to come on and fight (line 138)
- I ran after them (line 138)
- for the first time in my life I shouted at grownups (lines 140–141)
- I won the right (line 144)

Big Question page 41

Allow any well-supported answer. You may want to have students answer this question in the form of a debate, or by creating a T-chart with support for both opinions.

ASSESSMENT PRACTICE I: *p. 42*	
1. D	5. A
2. C	6. A
3. B	7. B
4. D	8. C

Point out to students that the test-taking strategies they learned as they read can be used with the following items:
- Item 5: change in a character (page 38)
- Items 7, 8: context clues (page 40)

The Rights to the Streets of Memphis

SECOND READ: CRITICAL ANALYSIS

If you are using this selection primarily for **test preparation**, direct students to preview the multiple choice questions on page 42 and the writing prompt on page 43 to help focus their reading. Explain that this technique may be used any time they take a reading test.

Analyze, page 37

Students might underline the following:

- stole upon me (line 1)
- had always been more or less at my elbow (lines 2–3)
- standing at my bedside, staring at me gauntly (line 4)
- grim, hostile stranger (line 5)
- feel hunger nudging my ribs (line 10)

Describing hunger as a person makes it seem more real and ominous. Wright finds hunger to be a threatening presence, and the reader gets the sense that he will have to fight it.

Draw Conclusions, page 38

Students might underline the following:

- "Where's your father?" (line 39)
- "I don't know" (line 45)
- "Who brings food into the house?" (line 46)
- "Papa," "He always brought food." (line 47)
- "Well, your father isn't here now" (line 48)
- "Where is he?" (line 49)
- "I don't know" (line 50)

Since the father has disappeared, the mother will be forced to earn money for the family alone. If she can find work at all, it will be for low wages, and she will not receive money from any outside sources. It will be up to her to keep the family from starving.

Draw Conclusions, page 38

Students might circle the following:

- I had been glad that he was not there (lines 42–43)
- image of my father became associated with my pangs of hunger (lines 53–54)
- deep biological bitterness (lines 54–55)

His father used to bring food into the house, but now he has abandoned the family and left them all hungry.

Classify, page 39

Students should check the box: *both*. Wright witnesses his mother's despair and is frightened by it, which is an external conflict. He also is afraid and confused because he doesn't quite understand what is going on but must take on adult responsibilities while his mother works, which is an internal conflict.

✓TestSmart page 39

Answer: A, ". . . should confront his fears." Students should underline line 81: "You've got to get over that . . . Now, go on."

Make Inferences, page 40

Wright's mother tells him that he has to get over his fears (line 81), indicating that the gang will continue to beat him unless he stands up to them. She says she is going to teach him to fight for himself (lines 98–99), which means that she also knows that he will have to deal with many of these kinds of issues alone since his father has disappeared.

✓TestSmart Vocabulary, page 40

Answer: B, unfriendly. Students may underline "gangs were after me," (lines 118–119) and "being beaten" (line 119).

Analyze, page 41

The external conflict, facing the gang, gives him inner strength because he is no longer afraid of the other boys. The internal struggle he is dealing with—being afraid and being forced to act like an adult while he is still a child—is resolved because he faces his fears, and the event propels him into adulthood.

Big Question page 41

Allow any well-supported answer. You may want to have students discuss this question in a large group and keep a tally of students' responses.

ASSESSMENT PRACTICE I: *p. 42*	
1. D	5. A
2. C	6. B
3. B	7. B
4. D	8. C

Point out to students that the test-taking strategies they learned as they read can be used with the following items:
- Items 2, 5: make an inference (page 39)
- Items 7, 8: context clues (page 40)

SHORT RESPONSE: OPINION Use this writing activity to determine whether students understand the nature of external and internal conflicts and the differences between them. Take them through the following steps:

- Have students analyze the prompt. They should notice that they are being asked to write one or two paragraphs.
- Tell them to fill out the chart, listing the external conflicts and then the internal conflicts.
- Students should go back to the text and circle details about the difficulty of Wright's external and internal conflicts.
- Last, tell students to state their opinion about which type of conflict was the biggest challenge for Wright and use the details they circled to support their answer.

TEST-TAKER'S TOOLKIT

EXTERNAL CONFLICTS

Wright is hungry.
Father has abandoned family.
Must take care of himself
Attacked by street gang
Mother won't let him back in house.

INTERNAL CONFLICTS

Angry with father
Confused by father's disappearance and mother's behavior
Forced to act like an adult while he's still a child
Must face fears of being beaten
Afraid of what mother will do if he comes home without groceries

SAMPLE OPINION

Wright had to face both internal and external conflicts. The greatest external conflict was dealing with the gang that had beaten him and stolen his grocery money. The biggest internal conflict was overcoming his own fears. I think the biggest challenge was the internal conflict because once he dealt with that, the external conflict was eliminated as well. When he says in line 122 that he "had a chance to fight and defend myself," he realizes that his only real choice is to stand up for himself. Once he succeeded in overcoming his fears in that situation, he knew he would be able to deal with other fears in the future.

SETTING A PURPOSE Complete the prereading activity on page 44 and review the teaching options below. Then share with your students what their goals will be, and use these goals to set a purpose for reading. Once students are clear on that purpose, have them write a purpose statement at the top of page 45.

TEST PREPARATION Direct students to read the multiple-choice questions on page 48, as well as the writing prompt on page 49, to help them focus their reading.

LEVEL 1

- ## Bullying Myths and Facts
- ## What Can You Do If Someone Is Bullying You?

FOCUS SKILL: PURPOSE AND AUDIENCE

ACTIVITY: SOLVE A PROBLEM

Before assigning the related readings, introduce the problem-solving chart and have students complete it in groups of four. The following day, ask them to revisit the chart and discuss whether they would do anything differently after reading the articles.

OPTIONS FOR TEACHING

SKILL INSTRUCTION Use "Learn the Skill" at the bottom of page 44 and page R2 in the Nonfiction Skills Handbook to review the focus skill of understanding purpose and audience.

> **ADDITIONAL RESOURCE:**
> **STANDARDS LESSON FILE: READING AND INFORMATIONAL TEXTS:** Determining Author's Purpose, page 23

JIGSAW LEARNING Divide the class into small groups, each responsible for learning and then sharing information about one of the following topics:
- definition and examples of bullying
- resources and strategies for dealing with bullies

If you are using Level 2 in the same classroom, add a third topic about the impact of discrimination and bullying on Richard Wright's life, and use "Books of the Times: *Black Boy*" as a resource.

DEBATE Have students debate whether the strategies for dealing with bullying might be applied to modern-day gangs as a way to counteract gang violence.

LEVEL 2

- ## Books of the Times: *Black Boy*

FOCUS SKILL: PURPOSE AND AUDIENCE

ACTIVITY: ANTICIPATION/REACTION GUIDE

Before assigning the related reading, introduce the response chart and have students fill in the first column with *Agree* and *Disagree*. After they have read the review, have them fill in the third column. Divide students into small groups and ask them to discuss their opinions.

OPTIONS FOR TEACHING

SKILL INSTRUCTION Use "Learn the Skill" at the bottom of page 44 and page R2 in the Nonfiction Skills Handbook to review the focus skill of understanding purpose and audience.

> **ADDITIONAL RESOURCE:**
> **STANDARDS LESSON FILE: READING AND INFORMATIONAL TEXTS:** Determining Author's Purpose, page 23

JIGSAW LEARNING Divide the class into small groups, each responsible for learning and then sharing information about one of the following topics:
- Life for African Americans in the South in the early 1900s; Students' research should focus on rights and laws (particularly Jim Crow laws).
- Combating the proliferation of gangs in urban areas

If you are using Level 1 in the same classroom, add "Bullying Myths & Facts" and "What Can You Do If Someone Is Bullying You?" to the list of resources in the second topic.

INVESTIGATION Have students investigate public response to Richard Wright's *Native Son*, *Black Boy*, or *American Hunger*.

Bullying Myths & Facts

Author's Purpose, page 45
Students should circle the subheadings "What is Bullying?" and "Bullying Myths and Facts." Students should check the first box: to inform.

Audience, page 45
Students should circle
- I went through it (lines 12–13)
- my kids (line 13)
- adults (line 18)
- peers (line 19)

The author is talking to both adults and children.

What Can You Do If Someone Is Bullying You?

Audience, page 46
Students should circle "It is NOT a normal part of growing up" (lines 8–9).

The audience is teenagers, because they are in the process of growing up.

Specialized Vocabulary, page 46
Students should underline the following:
- act upset or angry (line 26)
- act upset (line 28)

Evaluate, page 47
Students might circle
- Stand up, don't stand back (line 37)
- Refuse to join in . . . (line 42)
- Don't fight back (line 51)

✓**TestSmart** page 47

Answer: A, "to show readers how they can stop bullying"; Students should underline "Here are some things we all can do to stop bullying" (lines 10–12) and "Everyone has the right to be respected and the responsibility to respect others!" (lines 67–69).

ASSESSMENT PRACTICE II: *p. 48*	
1. A	5. D
2. B	6. D
3. B	7. B
4. A	8. A

Point out to students that the test-taking strategies they learned as they read can be used with the following item:
- Item 3: author's purpose (page 47)

Books of the Times: *Black Boy*

Author's Purpose, page 45
The author is writing to inform readers about Richard Wright's autobiography *Black Boy* and to offer criticism. The word *books* is in the title, and *dramatic, author,* and *story* are in the subheads. These words let readers know that the article is an in-depth book review.

Audience, page 45
Based on the author's tone and word choice, students might guess that the audience is probably white American adults. Students should circle "white Americans" (lines 29–30).

✓**TestSmart** page 46

Answer: D, "There will be a greater understanding . . ." Students should circle "If enough such books . . . millions of people read them" (lines 63–65).

Specialized Vocabulary, page 47
Possible response: "not able to be explained"

Evaluate, page 47
Possible response: Prescott seems to feel that Wright should have presented solutions for the harsh poverty and discrimination that he experienced. However, by describing the "mere filth" all around him, Wright's autobiography gave readers a view of a problem that many were unaware of, and it makes clear that Wright did whatever he had to in order to escape those surroundings. Wright's "thoughts and ideas" are apparent in the stark self-examination of his life.

Author's Purpose, page 47
Students may circle the following:
- it is powerful, moving, and horrifying (lines 158–159)
- certain to be extravagantly praised (line 160)
- It will be widely read. (lines 161–162)

Students may underline the following:
- emotionally dreadful (line 130)
- excessive determination . . . emphasize mere filth (lines 133–134)
- lack of artistic discrimination and selectivity (lines 135–136)
- little subtlety, little light and shade, no restraint (lines 154–155)

Prescott notes the power of Wright's writing in order to present a fair opinion of the book, instead of only pointing out what he considers the negative aspects. Prescott's audience is made up of people who want to be able to make an informed decision about the book, so they don't want to hear only one side of the argument.

ASSESSMENT PRACTICE II: *p. 48*	
1. A	5. D
2. D	6. A
3. A	7. C
4. C	8. B

Guide students through the steps described below under Guided Instruction. You may also wish to go over the rubric on the next page. (Consider modifying the rubric for these students, focusing only on Ideas, Organization, and Conventions.) Give students the entire 45 minutes to draft and review their responses. Point out, however, that in an actual timed writing situation, all steps of the writing process must be completed within the given time frame.

Share with students the rubric on the next page. Direct them to complete the entire writing process independently, within the actual 45-minute time frame they have been given.

GUIDED INSTRUCTION

ANALYZE THE PROMPT If necessary, lead students through the three-step analysis process on page 49. Explain that low scores are often the result of the writer missing a critical part of the directions. The marked prompt should look like this:

> In "The Rights to the Streets of Memphis" Richard Wright describes a defining moment in his life, when he stood up to a violent gang. <u>What childhood event was your defining moment?</u> Write an essay in which you (describe your defining moment) and (explain the effect it had on you.)

- You may want to point out that the last two sentences indicate that students should draw examples from their personal experience. This means students can use the pronoun *I*.
- As needed, guide students to understand that a **defining moment** is a life-changing moment, or one in which they feel they became who they are today. Tell them that while their essay will be personal, they are not required to write about anything they are uncomfortable sharing. Offer examples for them, such as a time when they gave a public speech, lost a ball game, or made friends with an unpopular person.
- Students might restate the prompt as "I am being asked to tell about an experience that made me who I am today, and to explain why it affected me as it did."

Remind students that the circled words and phrases should be addressed in their response.

PLAN YOUR RESPONSE

- Review with students the steps of a timed writing assignment. Analyze, Budget, Plan, Write. For a prompt like this, which requires them to describe a defining moment and explain its effect, remind them to budget enough time to explain its effect.
- Students should jot down vivid details in the chart. Point out, however, that in a real testing situation they would have had to supply the labels or headings for each section. Show them how the key words from the prompt suggested what those labels should be.

WRITE AND REVIEW Encourage students to try different voices in the first two or three sentences of their essay. When they have completed their draft, allow peers to comment on how well the students have met the requirements of the prompt.

RUBRIC FOR TIMED WRITING*

Key Traits	3 (Strong)	2 (Average)	1 (Weak)
IDEAS	• The writing centers around a clear and focused topic. • Vivid, well-chosen details support the key ideas.	• A topic is present, but it needs more development. • Some details support the key ideas.	• A clear topic is missing. • Details are missing or unclear.
ORGANIZATION	• The essay opens in an engaging way and wraps up with a satisfying conclusion. • The ideas flow in a logical manner.	• Both the introduction and the conclusion are vague and uninteresting. • Some transitional words and phrases are used, but more are needed.	• The essay has no real introduction or conclusion. • Transitions are not attempted.
VOICE	• The tone and voice are strongly individual and direct. • The tone is well-suited to the purpose and audience	• The tone and voice are flat at times. • The tone is sometimes inappropriate.	• The tone and voice lack an individual style. • The tone is completely inappropriate for the intended purpose and audience.
WORD CHOICE	• Words are lively, precise, and colorful. • The writer conveys meaning in a powerful, yet natural-sounding manner.	• Words are adequate and mostly correct. • Words and phrases communicate but are rarely memorable.	• Limited vocabulary and frequent mistakes impair understanding. • Vague words limit the meaning.
SENTENCE FLUENCY	• Sentences vary in length and structure and have a pleasing flow. • Sentence beginnings vary as appropriate to the topic and style.	• Sentences vary somewhat in length and structure, and some fragments and run-on sentences are present. • Sentence beginnings sometimes vary.	• Repetitive sentence structure, fragments, and run-on sentences make the writing difficult to follow. • Most or all sentences begin the same way.
CONVENTIONS	• Grammar and usage are correct. • Problems with mechanics (spelling, capitalization, and punctuation) are minor.	• Grammar and usage do not distort meaning but are not always correct. • Spelling, capitalization, and punctuation are uneven.	• Grammar and usage mistakes are frequent and distort meaning. • Spelling, capitalization, and punctuation are frequently incorrect.

*Use the Universal Rubric on the WriteSmart CD if you wish to further modify this chart.

The Necklace

by Guy de Maupassant

SUMMARY:

Written by Guy de Maupassant in 1884, "The Necklace" tells the story of a young woman's tragic pursuit of status. Madame Loisel, the wife of a clerk, borrows a diamond necklace to wear to an elegant party but then loses it. The Loisels replace the necklace, thus acquiring ten hard years of debt, only to learn later that the original necklace was a fake.

RELATED NONFICTION:

LEVEL 1

MAGAZINE ARTICLE: "How Far Would YOU Go to Fit In?"
This magazine article explores the question of status spending in teen culture. (*Readability*: Average)

LEVEL 2

MAGAZINE ARTICLE: "Money Really Can Buy Happiness"
This magazine article examines research studies that demonstrate why wealth and happiness are connected. (*Readability*: Challenging)

FOCUS AND MOTIVATE *p. 51*

FOR ALL STUDENTS

EXPLORE THE BIG QUESTION: *"How important is STATUS?"*
Discuss the question with students, encouraging them to consider how status affects the way they interact with family members, neighbors, and people in the school community. Ask students to name various types of status symbols. Then have them complete the Quickwrite in small groups. Ask volunteers to share their paragraphs with the class, and discuss as a whole group the value of things that determine status at your school.

INTRODUCE THE LESSON Tell students that in these selections, they will analyze the meaning and importance of status. Students in Level 1 will read an article about status spending in teen culture and status symbols throughout the ages. Students in Level 2 will read an article about the connection between money and happiness. Then call their attention to the Assessment Goals at the bottom of the page.

ASSESSMENT GOALS

LEVEL 1

- analyze character and point of view in a work of fiction
- use active reading strategies to comprehend text
- identify the main idea and supporting details of a nonfiction text
- analyze a writing prompt and plan a position paper

LEVEL 2

- analyze character and point of view in a work of fiction
- apply critical thinking skills to analyze text
- identify the main idea and supporting details of a nonfiction text
- analyze a writing prompt and plan a position paper

To help students understand character and point of view, begin by identifying a character trait, and challenge students to describe someone with that trait, without explicitly naming it. For example, they may portray a character who is insensitive as one who giggles uncontrollably when she sees someone trip and fall. Encourage students to use the three main methods of characterization in their descriptions:

- physical appearance
- the character's words, thoughts, and actions
- what others say about the character

Studying song lyrics can show the narrator's point of view. Have students share song lyrics they know and identify the narrator's point of view in each.

FIRST-PERSON POINT OF VIEW: Clues to first-person point of view are the words *I/we, me/us, my/our,* and *mine/ours.* A first-person song is the Beatles's "Can't Buy Me Love" ("**I** don't care too much . . . money can't buy **me** love").

THIRD-PERSON POINT OF VIEW: Clues to third-person point of view are the words *he/she/it/they, him/her/it/them,* and *his/hers/its/theirs.* A song in the third-person point of view is the Beatles's "Eleanor Rigby" ("All the lonely people / Where do **they** all come from?")

To review the ideas of point of view and character, make these points:

FOR FIRST-PERSON POINT OF VIEW

- The author can be the first-person narrator, but the narrator is not necessarily the author.
- First-person narrators are also given character traits by the author.
- First-person narrators may not be honest; they can lie or not tell all.
- A first-person narrator helps shape the reader's opinion of a character.

FOR THIRD-PERSON POINT OF VIEW

- A third-person narrator may address the reader.
- A third-person narrator is often more objective than a first-person narrator but still can affect the reader's opinion of a character.
- An author may choose a third-person narrator to distance the reader from the author because third-person narratives tend to feel less emotional.

ADDITIONAL TERMS FOR CRITICAL ANALYSIS

To reinforce understanding of **dynamic characters** and **static characters,** ask students to list three major characters from a movie or television show. Do these characters change? How?

FOR DYNAMIC AND STATIC CHARACTERS

- While most main characters and "good guys" are generally dynamic, minor characters and "bad guys" are usually static.
- Many things may happen in one episode to characters in television shows, but these characters often remain static.

ADDITIONAL RESOURCES
from McDougal Littell Literature

STUDENT'S EDITION
Literary Analysis Workshop, "Character and Point of View," p. 186
Additional selection questions, p. 218

STANDARDS LESSON FILE: LITERATURE
Lesson 1: Types of Characters and Character Traits, p. 1
Lesson 10: Narrator and First-Person Points of View, p. 87
Lesson 11: Narrator and Third-Person Points of View, p. 95

RESOURCE MANAGER
Selection Summary, p. 51
Additional Selection Questions, p. 47
Ideas for Extension, p. 48
Vocabulary Study, p. 57
Vocabulary Practice, p. 58
Reading Check, p. 60
Question Support, p. 61
Selection Test A, p. 65
Selection Test B/C, p. 67

BEST PRACTICES TOOLKIT
Analysis Frame: Character, pp. D26, D27
Follow the Character, p. D3
Character Analysis Chart, pp. D5, D50
Character Traits and Textual Evidence, pp. D6, D51
Character Traits Web, pp. D7, D52
Characters and Dialogue, pp. D8, D53

VOCABULARY IN CONTEXT Read aloud the context phrases below and show students how to use context clues to figure out meaning. Once students have offered their own suggestions, review the actual definitions.

SELECTION VOCABULARY

prospects *(n.)*: chances or possibilities, especially for financial success (line 2)

incessantly *(adv.)*: without interruption; continuously (line 12)

vexation *(n.)*: irritation; annoyance (line 42)

pauper *(n.)*: a poor person, especially one who depends on public charity (line 89)

adulation *(n.)*: excessive praise or flattery (line 125)

disconsolate *(adj.)*: extremely depressed or dejected (line 140)

aghast *(adj.)*: filled with shock or horror (line 163)

gamut *(n.)*: an entire range or series (line 195)

privation *(n.)*: the lack of a basic necessity or a comfort of life (line 199)

askew *(adj.)*: crooked; to one side (line 226)

CONTEXT PHRASES

1. better **prospects** of a good job after finishing college

2. whining and complaining **incessantly** about the work

3. the **vexation** caused by repeated misunderstandings

4. left the child a **pauper** who begged for coins in the street

5. appreciated the **adulation** and compliments on their project

6. felt completely **disconsolate** after losing the election

7. **aghast** that the mild librarian could even consider the crime

8. worked the **gamut** of jobs, from landscaping to waiting tables

9. the poor diet and shabby clothes typical of the **privations** of college students

10. wore the hat **askew** to cover the bug bite just above her eye

Make sure students are familiar with the following idioms that appear in this story.

- **come down in the world** (line 7): lost her status after having been prosperous
- **birth and breeding** (line 9): being born wealthy and well-educated
- **high society** (line 11): a group of wealthy or famous people
- **do them the honor** (line 50): demonstrate to them the respect; this is a polite way of extending an invitation
- **thrilled to death** (line 54): very excited

- **burst out** (line 59): said loudly
- **ill at ease** (line 86): uncomfortable
- **all out of sorts** (line 87): unhappy and distracted
- **in all her glory** (line 149): looking her best
- **her mind a blank** (lines 166–167): unable to think
- **drove him** (line 170): urged him, suggested he would be successful
- **stopped short** (line 258): stopped talking abruptly out of shock

The Necklace

CLOSE READ

If you are using this selection primarily for **test preparation,** direct students to preview the multiple choice questions on page 61 and the writing prompt on page 62 to help focus their reading. Explain that this technique may be used any time they take a reading test.

Pause & Reflect, page 54

1. MAKE INFERENCES To describe Madame Loisel's appearance, students might circle "pretty" (line 1) and "dressed plainly" (line 6).

To describe her feelings and desires they may underline
- unhappy (line 7)
- grieved incessantly, feeling that she had been born for all the little niceties and luxuries (lines 12–13)
- gnawed at her and made her furious (lines 16–17)
- roused in her disconsolate regrets and wild daydreams (line 18)
- dream of great reception halls hung with old silks, of fine furniture filled with priceless curios, and of small, stylish, scented sitting rooms (lines 23–25)
- distinguished and sought-after men whose attention every woman envies and longs to attract (lines 26–27)

If students underline "shabbiness," "dinginess," "worn-out," and "ugliness" (lines 13–15), explain that although these words are meant to describe Madame Liosel's surroundings, they also reflect how she feels.

Students should check *regretful* and *dissatisfied.*

2. DRAW CONCLUSIONS Possible response: Madame Loisel can't stand to be reminded of the difference between her dreary life and the way she wishes her life could be.

✓TestSmart page 55

Answer: D, "thrifty"; Students should underline "one you could wear for other affairs too" (line 73).

Connect, page 55

Students' responses will vary. Some students may explain that they sympathize more with Madame Loisel because they can understand her feeling that she deserves more out of life. Other students may sympathize with Monsieur Loisel because even though he tries to make her happy, she only becomes more disappointed with her situation, and he knows he will never be able to give her much more.

Pause & Reflect, page 56

1. MAKE INFERENCES Possible response: Monsieur Loisel doesn't know or care enough about status symbols to understand that flowers would identify his wife as a member of the working class, and he thinks she is foolish for caring. Madame Loisel is so status-conscious that she would be ashamed if she felt that other, wealthier women were looking down on her because she couldn't afford fine things.

2. CLARIFY Students should underline:
- her pulse beat faster with longing (line 110)
- Her hands trembled (line 110)
- she stood in ecstasy (lines 111–112)

Possible response: Madame Loisel believes that the diamond necklace is most likely to make her appear wealthy and thus fit in at the party. She may feel that it represents her true worth.

✓TestSmart Vocabulary, page 57

Answer: B, "outer garments such as a shawl or coat"

Clarify, page 57

Students should check *third-person omniscient.*

Possible response: Madame Loisel is tired from a long night and depressed because the most exciting night of her life has come to an end. She concentrates on the past and things that might have been. Monsieur Loisel is tired and disappointed to be walking home at sunrise, since in just a few hours he has to be at work, as always. He lives in the present.

Pause & Reflect, page 58

PREDICT Possible responses: The Loisels will keep looking for the necklace, will try to replace the necklace, or will admit to Madame Forestier that they lost the necklace. Accept any answer that can be supported by the students' analysis of the Loisels' character traits.

Monitor & Evaluate, page 59

Students may underline:
- scouring the grease from pots and pans (line 213)
- scrubbed dirty linen, shirts, and cleaning rags (lines 213–214)
- took the garbage down to the street (lines 214–215)

Students' responses will vary. Students who are not surprised may say that Madame Loisel's education and pride motivate her to do the right thing. *Remediation Tip:* Students who are surprised might suggest that Madame Loisel was dissatisfied with her previous lifestyle, and so she should complain more now that she must work. Point out that her character traits, especially her desire to belong to a higher class, demand that she honor her debts and protect her and her husband's reputation, as anyone from a higher class would try to do. It is more important to her that they keep what little they own than lose it all because they can't repay their debts.

Visualize, page 59

Students should underline
- appeared an old woman (line 225)
- heavy, rough, harsh, like one of the poor . . . hair untended, her skirts askew, her hands red (lines 225–227)

Some students may find that their visualization of Madame Loisel is helped by "voice shrill," "slopped water on her floors and scrubbed them herself" (lines 227–228); and "she would sit near the window and think" (lines 228–229) because of the added insight into her thoughts and actions.

Pause & Reflect, page 60

1. DRAW CONCLUSIONS Possible response: Madame Loisel responds this way because she has learned humility. She is proud of herself for having kept the secret and worked off the debt, joyful that her friend never missed the original necklace, and pleased that her ordeal is now over.

2. MAKE JUDGMENTS Student responses will vary. Students may have different ideas about what a "good ending" might be; if so, ask them if the ending is logical, based on what they now know about the characters. Accept any answer that thoughtfully takes into account Madame Loisel's character traits and motivations.

Big Question page 60

Possible response: Guy de Maupassant wrote the story to illustrate that status is just as much of an illusion as a fake diamond necklace, and that chasing it can cost a person time, money, and happiness. Students may cite lines 9–11 (Their natural poise . . . the equals of ladies in high society) if they suggest that the author believes that people are truly equal. You may want to have students create a T-chart that lists the actions that Monsieur Loisel was willing to take in the interest of status versus those Madame Loisel was willing to take.

ASSESSMENT PRACTICE I: *p. 61*	
1. B	5. A
2. C	6. D
3. A	7. D
4. B	8. A

Point out to students that the test-taking strategies they learned as they read can be used with the following items:
• Item 2: identify character traits (page 55)
• Item 7: multiple-meaning words (page 57)

The Necklace

SECOND READ: CRITICAL ANALYSIS

If you are using this selection primarily for **test preparation**, direct students to preview the multiple choice questions on page 61 and the writing prompt on page 62 to help focus their reading. Explain that this technique may be used any time they take a reading test.

Analyze, page 53

Students should underline "pretty" (line 1) and "dressed plainly" (line 6) for words and phrases that describe Madame Loisel's appearance. Students should circle "unhappy" (line 7) as the word that describes her emotional state.

Possible response: The author has revealed that Madame Loisel feels that she was born for a better life than the one she has as the wife of a clerk. These feelings cause her to go to great lengths to give the appearance of being wealthy at the party.

Compare & Evaluate, page 54

Students should underline lines 29–31 (opposite her husband . . . nothing I like better).

Student responses will vary. Students may point out that Madame Loisel is the main, and more complex, character, who must be understood in the beginning for later changes to be appreciated. Some may note that though the description of Monsieur Loisel is concise, readers nevertheless learn a great deal about him and what he values.

Connect, page 54

Accept any well-supported answer, as students will have their own perceptions of the importance of status. They may answer that as Madame Loisel's friend, they would advise her to pay less attention to her social status so that they can both enjoy their friendly visits together. Her wishes will cause her trouble one day.

Contrast, page 55

Students should underline "proudly holding out a large envelope" (lines 44–45) and "scornfully tossed the invitation on the table" (lines 52–53).

Possible response: Monsieur Loisel is simple, yet proud of his accomplishments, but Madame Loisel is unappreciative, self-centered, and too overly concerned about her appearance to look forward to the event.

Interpret, page 56

Possible response: Madame Loisel's self-consciousness about her status motivates her to borrow the jewelry. She would be ashamed if she felt that other, wealthier women were looking down on her because she couldn't afford fine things. She has similar motives for her hasty escape from the party—her shabby wraps would alert other women to her true social position.

Evaluate, page 56

Most students will say that Madame Loisel's opinion about the value of status has been strengthened. At the party she is lavished with attention by members of the elite class, who likely believe she is one of them. *Remediation tip:* Students who say that her opinion has been weakened may cite the text that says both she and her husband are disconsolate on their trip home. Point out that this is because they are cold and tired. Madame Loisel may also realize that she will be able to attend few, if any, such parties in the future. Discuss whether a tiny taste of what a person cannot have is more tortuous than having none at all.

✓ TestSmart page 57

Answer: D, "third-person omniscient"; *Remediation Tip:* Some students may answer that the story is written from the third-person limited point of view because the narrator writes mainly from Madame Loisel's perspective. Point out that the lines about Monsieur Loisel's plans to purchase a hunting rifle (lines 80–82) are his thoughts and could only have come from an omniscient narrator. Monsieur Loisel is not the main character, but his thoughts are known to the narrator.

✓ TestSmart page 58

Answer: B, "a fastening device"

Classify, page 59

Students should answer that Madame Loisel is a dynamic character. Students' explanations will vary, but they should cite line 208 (sudden heroism) and line 211 (She learned to . . .) as examples of how the author indicates the changes that occur in her character.

Make Judgments, page 59

Possible response: The reader can tell that Monsieur Loisel is a static character because he is introduced as a simple, frugal, hard-working man and remains so throughout the ten years it takes the couple to work their way out of debt. Students may also point out that, from the time Loisel declares, "We must take steps to replace that piece of jewelry" (lines 178–179), the author leaves his presence out of the rest of the story, suggesting that his character is constant.

Interpret, page 60

Student responses will vary. Students may cite line 261 ("she smiled with proud and simple joy") and line 239 ("now that everything was paid off, she would tell her the whole story") to explain that Madame Loisel was proud that she had acted honorably, even though she had suffered ten years to replace the necklace. Students might also suggest that, due to the growth of her character, Madame Loisel hoped her friend would praise her hard work and responsibility as she had once longed for people to praise her for frivolous things such as dresses and jewels.

Big Question page 60

Accept any well-supported answer. Some may say that status has the greatest impact on the story because fate only presents the characters with circumstance, whereas the characters' status-consciousness causes them to react to those circumstances in ways that change their lives forever. Monsieur Loisel received the invitation mostly by chance, and his wife might have chosen to attend in the dress she wears to the theater if she weren't so concerned with her image. Students who believe that fate had the greater impact may cite the fact that the necklace falling off was mere chance, yet it dramatically altered the lives of two people.

ASSESSMENT PRACTICE I: *p. 61*	
1. B	5. D
2. C	6. C
3. A	7. D
4. B	8. A

Point out to students that the test-taking strategies they learned as they read can be used with the following items:
- Item 1: identify point of view (page 57)
- Item 7: multiple-meaning words (page 58)

SHORT RESPONSE: CHARACTER SKETCH Use this writing activity to determine whether students understand characterization through identifying motivation and character traits. Take them through the following steps:

- Have students analyze the prompt. They should notice that they are being asked to write a character sketch. As needed, point out the explanation of *character sketch* in the Test-Taker's Toolkit.

- Tell them to fill out the chart, listing the character's physical traits, personality traits, and motivations. Suggest that they go back to the text and circle descriptions of Madame or Monsieur Loisel that indicate traits, as well as clues that suggest motivations.

- Lastly, tell students to create a sketch that gives a clear, complete picture of the character they chose, using the details they circled to support their description.

TEST-TAKER'S TOOLKIT

PHYSICAL TRAITS	PERSONALITY TRAITS	CHARACTER MOTIVATIONS
early in the story: pretty	can be charming	She believes she was meant to be wealthy.
later in the story: appeared old, heavy, harsh	doesn't appreciate what she has honorable	She works hard to pay her debt.

SAMPLE CHARACTER SKETCH

CHARACTER STUDY OF: MADAME LOISEL

Madame Loisel is described as being pretty and charming, but she is unhappy. She concentrates on wealth and is distressed that she will never be rich or have the things that rich people have. She does not appreciate what she has. For example, when her husband brings home an invitation to a party, she is only more upset because she feels she has nothing decent to wear. She is mostly motivated by desire for the life she can't have. One good feature is that she is honorable and is willing to work when she loses her friend's necklace and needs to replace it.

SETTING A PURPOSE Complete the prereading activity on page 63 and review the teaching options below. Then share with your students what their goals will be, and use these goals to set a purpose for reading. Once students are clear on that purpose, have them write a purpose statement at the top of page 64.

TEST PREPARATION Direct students to read the multiple-choice questions on page 68, as well as the writing prompt on page 69, to help them focus their reading.

LEVEL 1

• How Far Would YOU Go to Fit In?

FOCUS SKILL: IDENTIFY MAIN IDEA AND DETAILS

ACTIVITY: SELF-SURVEY

Before assigning the related readings, introduce the Self-Survey and have students complete it individually and discuss it in pairs. The following day, ask them to revisit the survey and discuss whether they would change their answers after reading the article.

OPTIONS FOR TEACHING

SKILL INSTRUCTION Use "Learn the Skill" at the bottom of page 63 and page R2 in the Nonfiction Skills Handbook to review the focus skill of identifying main idea and details.

> **ADDITIONAL RESOURCES:**
>
> **STANDARDS LESSON FILE: READING AND INFORMATION TEXTS:** Recognizing Main Idea and Details, page 33

JIGSAW LEARNING Divide the class into small groups. Assign each one of the following topics:
- status symbols for present-day American teens
- features of advertising that are aimed at teenagers

If you are using Level 2 in the same classroom, add a third topic about the influence of money on teens' happiness, and use "Money Really Can Buy Happiness" as a resource.

SURVEY Have groups create surveys to pass out to classmates. Questions on the survey could include: what status symbols do you feel you must have? How much will you pay for them? How much do you spend now? Where do you get spending money? Answers can be tallied and the results presented to the class.

LEVEL 2

• Money Really Can Buy Happiness

FOCUS SKILL: IDENTIFY MAIN IDEA AND DETAILS

ACTIVITY: LIST THE PROS AND CONS

Before assigning the related reading, introduce the response chart and have students fill in the first column with *Money's Positive Effects* and the second column with *Money's Negatives Effects*. After they have read the article, divide students into small groups and ask them to discuss their opinions.

OPTIONS FOR TEACHING

SKILL INSTRUCTION Use "Learn the Skill" at the bottom of page 63 and page R2 in the Nonfiction Skills Handbook to review the focus skill of identifying main ideas and details.

> **ADDITIONAL RESOURCES:**
>
> **STANDARDS LESSON FILE: READING AND INFORMATION TEXTS:** Recognizing Main Idea and Details, page 33

JIGSAW LEARNING Divide the class into small groups, each responsible for learning and then sharing information about one of the following topics:
- changes in leisure time for Americans in the last 50 years
- sources of income for teenage Americans
- types of status symbols for American teenagers

If you are using Level 1 in the same classroom, add "How Far Would YOU Go to Fit In?" to the list of resources in the third topic.

INVESTIGATION Have students investigate teenage spending habits and surveys measuring their happiness in different countries around the world.

How Far Would YOU Go to Fit In?

Preview, page 64
Possible response: Many young people have an obsession with status that can lead to problems. Some students may be helped by a review of the "Learn the Skill" feature, particularly the information about examples and anecdotes.

Specialized Vocabulary, page 65
Students should underline the following:
• Advertisers spend . . . $15 billion (lines 17–18)
• kids have buying power (line 23)
Possible definition: **market** *(v.)*: to spend money to present information about products to customers who want and can afford them
Word Analysis *(v.)*: 1. To offer for sale; 2. To sell

Main Idea and Details, page 65
Answers: statistics, graphics
Possible response: Teens have a lot of money to spend, and they are spending more every year.

✓**TestSmart** page 66
Answer: B, "Many teens base what they buy on fear rather than desire." Students should underline "being ridiculed at school teaches teens" (lines 47–48). *Remediation Tip:* Ask students who underline "cool kids can't always tell the difference" (line 50) if not being able to tell the difference between what you want and what you have been told to want is the same thing as being afraid.

Connect, page 66
Students' responses will vary. Some students may say that they don't think much about why they buy the things they do. Suggest that they think back to a recent clothing, electronics, or other purchase that they made, and ask them to try to remember what they were thinking when they made the decision to buy the item.

✓**TestSmart** page 67
Answer: D, "Status symbols of the past include pearls, jade, and silk."

Evaluate, page 67
Accept any well-reasoned response. Ask students who agree with the last sentence what activities might take the place of status-chasing for young people. Ask students who disagree what positive effects spending money on status symbols has had on their lives.

ASSESSMENT PRACTICE II: *p. 68*	
1. B	5. C
2. A	6. A
3. C	7. A
4. B	8. D
Point out to students that the test-taking strategies they learned as they read can be used with the following item: • Item 2: identify main idea (page 66)	

Money Really Can Buy Happiness

Preview, page 64
Possible response: Research provides evidence of a connection between wealth and happiness.

Monitor, page 65
Students should underline:
• love and good health (line 45)
• sense of belonging and purpose (line 46)
• things . . . inextricably linked to how much money you have (lines 48–49)

Main Idea and Details, page 65
Students should check *facts, expert testimony,* and *examples.*

Specialized Vocabulary, page 66
Possible definition: describing or relating to the pursuit of pleasure and material happiness

✓**TestSmart** page 66
Answer: C, "people can't always recall their feelings accurately"; *Remediation tip:* If some students chose another answer, suggest that they look in the text to see if a sentence or phrase has very nearly the same meaning as one of the answer choices. They should see that the sentence in lines 83–85 (It's extremely hard for most people to accurately remember . . .) is similar to the correct answer choice.

Specialized Vocabulary, page 67
Students should underline:
• came into inheritance or a lottery win (lines 100–101)
• came into money (line 103)
• as little as £1,000 (line 104)
• a win of £1.5 million or more (lines 105–106)
Students might generate a definition of *windfall* as a sudden occurrence that increases a person's wealth.
Word Analysis 1. *(n.)* A sudden, unexpected piece of good fortune or personal gain

Connect, page 67
Accept any well-reasoned response. You may want to suggest that students consider whether those who are wealthy truly appreciate what they have.

ASSESSMENT PRACTICE II: *p. 68*	
1. A	5. B
2. D	6. C
3. D	7. D
4. B	8. B

LEVEL 1

Guide students through the steps described below under Guided Instruction. You may also wish to go over the rubric on the next page. (Consider modifying the rubric for these students, focusing only on Ideas, Organization, and Conventions.) Give students the entire 30 minutes to draft and review their responses. Point out, however, that in an actual timed writing situation, all steps of the writing process must be completed within the given time frame.

LEVEL 2

Share with students the rubric on the next page. Direct them to complete the entire writing process independently, within the actual 30-minute time frame they have been given.

GUIDED INSTRUCTION

ANALYZE THE PROMPT Lead students through the three-step analysis process on page 69. Tell them low scores are often the result of missing a critical part of the directions. The marked prompt should look like this:

> Characters such as Madame Loisel are overly concerned with status. Some people, however, claim to have no interest in their own status, or in anyone else's. Such people say they judge others based on their actions and personality. <u>Do you think it is possible to ignore status?</u> Write a (position paper) to explain (your views) on this question. Support your position with (examples from the readings) and (from your own experiences).

- You may want to point out that the last two sentences indicate that students should draw examples from their views and personal experience.
- As needed, prompt students to identify a specific time in their lives when they either judged others based on status or ignored someone else's status. Encourage students to use alternate names if they are using their classmates as examples.
- *Academic Vocabulary*: Students are asked to write a **position paper**, so they need to state and explain their views on the topic. Then remind students that the circled words and phrases should be addressed in their response if they want to achieve the highest score on the test.

PLAN YOUR RESPONSE

- Review with students the steps of a timed writing assignment. For a prompt like this, requiring them to support a position with examples, remind them to budget enough time to find the examples.
- Students should jot down examples in the chart. Point out, however, that in a real testing situation they would have had to plan the organization of their own writing.

WRITE AND REVIEW Students may wish to write two or three opening sentences based on the suggestions, and ask a classmate to choose the best one. Peers may also comment on how well a student's draft meets the requirements of the prompt before the student revises the draft.

RUBRIC FOR TIMED WRITING*

Key Traits	3 (Strong)	2 (Average)	1 (Weak)
IDEAS	• The thesis statement is focused and clearly identifies the issue and the writer's position. • Relevant details and examples support each key idea. • The writer clearly explains how the examples are relevant to the position.	• The thesis statement is too broad or too narrow but loosely identifies the issue and the writer's position. • Most key ideas are supported by details and examples. • The writer usually explains how the examples are relevant to the position.	• The thesis statement is unclear or missing. • Details and examples are not relevant or are too scarce to support the key ideas. • The writer does not explain how the examples are relevant to the thesis.
ORGANIZATION	• The introduction clearly presents the issue and draws the reader in. • The conclusion summarizes the ideas. • Transitional words and phrases clearly show how ideas connect. • The organization is logical and follows a consistent pattern.	• The introduction presents the issue, but it does not draw the reader in. • The conclusion summarizes some ideas. • Most of the transitions work, but a few more are needed. • The organization shows some logic but does not follow a consistent pattern.	• The introduction does not clearly set up what the essay is about. • The essay lacks an identifiable conclusion. • The writer uses few, if any, transitional words. • The organization feels random or disjointed; the reader often feels lost or confused.
VOICE	• The tone and voice are appropriate for the purpose and audience. • The writing reflects active engagement with the topic.	• The tone and voice are acceptable for the purpose and audience but not strongly individual or direct. • The writing lacks consistent engagement with the topic.	• The voice lacks individuality and is not concerned with or not matched to the audience. • The writing reflects no engagement with the topic.
WORD CHOICE	• Words and phrases are used effectively. • Logic is sound, and appeals to emotion are appropriate.	• Words are adequate and mostly correct. • Some errors in logic and inappropriate appeals to emotion are present.	• Limited vocabulary and/or frequent misuse of parts of speech impair understanding. • Frequent errors in logic and inappropriate appeals to emotion distract the reader.
SENTENCE FLUENCY	• Sentences vary in length and structure. • Sentence beginnings are varied.	• Sentences do not significantly vary in structure, and some fragments and run-on sentences are present. • Sentence beginnings are mostly the same.	• Repetitive sentence structure, fragments, and run-on sentences make the writing difficult to follow. • Most or all sentences begin the same way.
CONVENTIONS	• Spelling, capitalization, and punctuation are generally correct. • Grammar and usage are correct. • Paragraphing tends to be correct and reinforces the organization.	• Spelling, capitalization, and punctuation are sometimes uneven. • Grammar and usage do not distort meaning but are not always correct. • Paragraphing is attempted but is not always sound.	• Spelling, capitalization, and punctuation are frequently incorrect. • Grammar and usage mistakes are frequent and distort meaning. • Paragraphing is missing, irregular, or too frequent.

*Use the Persuasive Essay Rubric on the WriteSmart CD if you wish to further modify this chart.

The Cask of Amontillado

by Edgar Allan Poe

SUMMARY:

"The Cask of Amontillado" is Edgar Allan Poe's classic tale of revenge. Montresor, the narrator of this dark short story, tricks Fortunato into accompanying him to the burial vaults beneath his palace, where Montresor stores his wine. Once there, Montresor leads the inebriated Fortunato deep into the catacombs and then walls him up inside a crypt, leaving him there to die.

RELATED NONFICTION:

`LEVEL 1`

BOOK EXCERPT: "Where Corpses End Up"
This book excerpt traces the history and purposes of catacombs and describes how modern visitors respond to these ancient burial sites. (*Readability*: Average)

BOOK EXCERPT: "Guerilla Literature: Plotting the Horror Short Story"
This book excerpt explores how and why writers of horror fiction ply their craft. (*Readability*: Easy)

`LEVEL 2`

NEWSPAPER ARTICLE: "He Who Cast the First Stone Probably Didn't"
What's a fair response to a wrong? Research on the psychology that underlies revenge, retaliation, and retribution is presented in this newspaper article. (*Readability*: Challenging)

FOCUS AND MOTIVATE *p. 71*

`FOR ALL STUDENTS`

EXPLORE THE BIG QUESTION: *"Is REVENGE ever justified?"*
Discuss the question with students, and invite them to provide scenarios in which revenge might be reasonable or appropriate. Encourage them to consider the possible drawbacks of revenge. Then have them complete the **Chart It** activity with a partner, and compare their responses with another pair.

INTRODUCE THE LESSON Tell students that in these selections, they will explore the idea of revenge and how people respond to fear. Students in Level 1 will read two book excerpts on situations that can cause fear. Students in Level 2 will read about the psychological workings behind revenge and retaliation. Then call their attention to the Assessment Goals at the bottom of the page.

ASSESSMENT GOALS

`LEVEL 1`

- analyze setting, mood, and imagery in a work of fiction
- use active reading strategies to comprehend text
- identify the flow of ideas in nonfiction texts
- analyze a writing prompt and plan a response to literature

`LEVEL 2`

- analyze setting, mood, and imagery in a work of fiction
- apply critical thinking skills to analyze text
- examine the flow of ideas in nonfiction texts
- analyze a writing prompt and plan a response to literature

LEVEL 1

Explain that details about a setting can build and contribute to a mood. Use the following scenarios to help students understand how setting can influence mood.

Scenario 1: Help students visualize having a picnic with a friend in a meadow on a sunny day. On a hike after lunch, they come across what looks like a pleasant, abandoned cottage that they decide to explore. Elicit from students details about the setting they are envisioning in their minds. Then ask students to tell how the setting makes them feel. List their responses on the board under the headings *Setting* and *Mood*.

Scenario 2: Now help students imagine that they have been hiking with a friend through a meadow and a severe thunderstorm has hit. They see what looks like an abandoned cottage and decide they have to take shelter there from the storm. Elicit details about this setting and how these details make them feel. List these responses under the headings on the board.

Compare students' responses to each scenario and elicit that one setting, with different details, can create very dissimilar moods. Use the two scenarios to discuss how setting can affect plot, and ask what might happen next in each scenario.

LEVEL 2

If helpful, review the definitions of **setting, mood,** and **imagery.** You may wish to include these additional points:

FOR SETTING

- Setting may play an active role in a story by creating or adding to a conflict.
- Characters may make decisions or behave in a particular way as a direct result of the setting.

FOR IMAGERY AND MOOD

- The sensory images a writer presents are often integral to shaping the story's mood.
- Just a few strong sensory images allow the reader's imagination to fill in the rest of a scene.

ADDITIONAL TERMS FOR CRITICAL ANALYSIS

To highlight the difference between **dramatic irony** and **verbal irony,** direct students' attention to the first paragraph of "The Cask of Amontillado," and point out that the narrator lets the reader in on his secret plan for Fortunato immediately. This example of dramatic irony

- sets up a relationship between the narrator and the reader
- establishes circumstances for verbal irony to occur

ADDITIONAL RESOURCES
from **McDougal Littell Literature**

STUDENT'S EDITION
Literary Analysis Workshop, "Setting, Mood, and Imagery," p. 302
Additional selection questions, p. 353

STANDARDS LESSON FILE: LITERATURE
Lesson 9: Setting and Its Roles, p. 77
Lesson 28: Imagery, p. 265
Lesson 38: Verbal and Dramatic Irony, p. 359
Lesson 44: Mood, p. 417

RESOURCE MANAGER
Selection Summary, p. 77
Additional Selection Questions, p. 73
Ideas for Extension, p. 74
Vocabulary Study, p. 83
Vocabulary Practice, p. 84
Reading Check, p. 86
Question Support, p. 87
Selection Test A, p. 91
Selection Test B/C, p. 93

BEST PRACTICES TOOLKIT
Setting Diagram, pp. D12, D57
Analysis Frame: Setting, p. D30

PRETEACH VOCABULARY

VOCABULARY IN CONTEXT: Read aloud the context phrases below and show students how to use context clues to figure out meaning. Once students have offered their own suggestions, review the actual definitions.

SELECTION VOCABULARY

preclude *(v.)*: to make impossible, especially by taking action in advance (line 6)
impunity *(n.)*: freedom from penalty or harm (line 7)
immolation *(n.)*: death or destruction (line 13)
abscond *(v.)*: to go away suddenly and secretly (line 61)
repose *(v.)*: to lie dead or at rest (line 98)
termination *(n.)*: an end, limit, or edge (line 153)
subside *(v.)*: to decrease in amount or intensity; settle down (line 184)
aperture *(n.)*: an opening, such as a hole or a gap (line 219)

CONTEXT PHRASES

1. to **preclude** pain

2. to lie with **impunity**

3. **immolation** of an enemy

4. **abscond** with money

5. everlasting **repose**

6. **termination** of a job

7. to help anger to **subside**

8. to close off an **aperture**

FOR ENGLISH LEARNERS

Make sure students are familiar with the following terms and references that appear in this story.

Idioms Review and discuss the following expressions with students.

- **at his heels** (line 157): behind him
- **in a great measure** (line 177): mostly
- **worn off** (line 177): gone away

Cultural References Review the following terms used in nineteenth-century America with students.

- **Sherry** (line 56): a common Spanish wine
- **attendants** (line 61): servants

The Cask of Amontillado

CLOSE READ

If you are using this selection primarily for **test preparation,** direct students to preview the multiple choice questions on page 80 and the writing prompt on page 81 to help focus their reading. Explain that this technique may be used any time they take a reading test.

Monitor, page 74

Students may underline "dusk, one evening" (line 23) and "carnival season" (line 24). Possible responses: Fortunato has been drinking; he is wearing a costume. If students offer other responses, ask them to show support from the text.

Make Inferences, page 74

The narrator has no real interest in what Fortunato thinks of his wine. Students should note that Montresor has previously explained in lines 14–16 that Fortunato's weakness is his pride in his knowledge of wine, and since Montresor is planning to get revenge, it is unlikely that he cares about Fortunato's opinion of his Amontillado.

Pause & Reflect, page 75

DRAW CONCLUSIONS Students should check the words *suspenseful* and *tense.* If students choose other responses, ask them to explain their reasoning.

Pause & Reflect, page 76

EVALUATE Students should underline the descriptions in lines 104–105 and the motto in line 107. Both the arms and the motto fit Montresor's personality very well. If needed, refer students back to Montresor's declarations in the first paragraph of the story. *Remediation Tip:* Have students guide you to make a sketch of the coat of arms on the board, and discuss how this image and the motto support each other.

✔TestSmart Vocabulary, page 77

Answer: B, "a drink"; Students may underline "the Medoc" (line 118), and "emptied it at a breath" (lines 119–120).

Visualize, page 77

Sensory descriptions help readers visualize the journey the two men make. Students might underline the following words and phrases:
- leaned upon it heavily (line 137)
- a range of low arches (line 138)
- descended . . . descending again (lines 138–139)
- foulness of the air . . . to glow than flame (line 140)

Students should check *gloomy.*

Pause & Reflect, page 78

1. *CLARIFY* Montresor has chained him to a granite wall in the innermost part of the crypt. Students should underline "fettered him to the granite" (lines 159–160), "Throwing the links . . . to secure it" (lines 162–163).
2. *PREDICT* To take revenge, Montresor will leave Fortunato chained there to die. As needed, guide students to use details from the text to support their predictions.

Visualize, page 78

Students might underline the following phrases:
- low moaning cry (line 178)
- furious vibrations of the chain (line 181)
- clanking subsided (lines 183–184)
- a few feeble rays (line 187)

Ask students to determine which sense most of these phrases appeal to. Discuss how descriptions of sounds can be effective in suspenseful scenes.

✔TestSmart page 79

Answer: C, "to show Fortunato . . . no one can hear them." Students should underline line 192, in which Montresor reminds himself that the catacombs' walls are very thick.

Pause & Reflect, page 79

CLARIFY Montresor's plan succeeds; students should underline "For the half of a century no mortal has disturbed them" (line 224). Students should circle "My heart grew sick" in line 221 to support the response that he does not feel completely content with his actions.

Big Question page 79

Responses may include a range of opinions. Allow any well-supported answer. Invite students to reflect on the fact that 50 years after his terrible deed, Montresor has written this highly detailed account of what he did.

ASSESSMENT PRACTICE I: *p. 80*	
1. B	5. C
2. A	6. B
3. D	7. B
4. C	8. C
Point out to students that the test-taking strategies they learned as they read can be used with the following items: • Item 6: make inferences (page 79) • Item 7: multiple-meaning words (page 77)	

The Cask of Amontillado

SECOND READ: CRITICAL ANALYSIS

If you are using this selection primarily for **test preparation**, direct students to preview the multiple choice questions on page 80 and the writing prompt on page 81 to help focus their reading. Explain that this technique may be used any time they take a reading test.

Analyze, page 73
Students should note that Montresor not only plans to get his revenge, but that he also does not intend to get caught. He will not give Fortunato any indication of what is in store for him. As needed, guide students to paraphrase the dense, formal language of the opening paragraphs.

Students may offer differing opinions about when, towards the end of the story, Fortunato finally understands his fate. Some may think that it comes when Montresor is walling up the niche and Fortunato screams and yells (line 188); others may think that Fortunato holds out hope that it is a "jest" until about line 212. Encourage them to support their ideas with evidence from the text.

Draw Conclusions, page 74
Students should circle "carnival season" (line 24). The setting influences the plot in several ways: it influences Fortunato to drink in celebration, thereby impairing his judgment and abilities; it allows the servants at the palazzo to be out; it engenders feelings of good will that Montresor exploits to his advantage.

Analyze, page 74
Students should note that the verbal irony adds to the suspenseful mood because it shows the reader, who knows Montresor's plan, that Montresor's ideas about Fortunato's shortcomings are correct. Some responses may also indicate that the suspense is heightened because the reader begins to feel sympathetic towards Fortunato.

Analyze, page 75
Possible response: The setting has moved from the loud, bright merriment of the carnival to the dark, damp catacombs. This changes the mood from one of merriment to one that is more sinister.

Reason Inductively, page 75
Students might underline the following details:
- The gait of my friend was unsteady (line 71)
- two filmy orbs . . . rheum of intoxication (lines 76–77)
- My poor friend . . . for many minutes. (line 82)

Students' opinions about Fortunato may differ but should show good reasoning. A possible response: Fortunato becomes more sympathetic as he changes from being loud and somewhat arrogant to a person who is clearly in great peril and unlikely to be able to defend himself.

Classify, page 76
Among the examples students might mark are the following:
- "You are a man to be missed." (line 86)
- "you should use all proper caution" (line 91)
- "(I drink) to your long life" (line 99)

The dialogue here affords an opportunity to discuss the difference between dramatic irony and verbal irony. Many of Montresor's speeches are examples of verbal irony. Fortunato's words are not delivered in an ironic way, but the secret the reader is in on renders the situation ironic.

Visualize & Interpret, page 76
Students' drawings should reflect the description in lines 104–105. Possible response: The image represents exactly what Montresor plans for Fortunato—to kill him in response to an injury.

✓ **TestSmart** **Vocabulary**, page 77
Answer: B, "a drink"; Students may underline "the Medoc" (line 118), and "emptied it at a breath" (lines 119–120).

Monitor, page 77
For sensory imagery relating to sight, students may cite any one of the vivid descriptions of things seen in the crypt, such as the description of the niter (lines 114–116). For touch, students may cite "leaned upon it heavily" (line 137). For smell, students may cite "the foulness of the air" (lines 139–140).

Analyze, page 78
Students should explain that Montresor's words are ironic because he "implore(s)" Fortunato to leave after he has chained him to the wall.

Interpret, page 78
Students might underline the following:
- low moaning cry (line 178)
- furious vibrations of the chain (line 181)
- clanking subsided (lines 183–184)
- a few feeble rays (line 187)

Possible response: The descriptions highlight Fortunato's growing realization about his situation and add to a mood of impending doom. Point out that Fortunato's frenzied efforts are juxtaposed with Montresor's calm demeanor as he lays the bricks that will wall Fortunato in.

✓ **TestSmart** page 79
Answer: C, "to show Fortunato . . . no one can hear them." Students should underline line 192, in which Montresor reminds himself that the walls are very thick.

Big Question page 79
Allow any well-supported answer. Some may feel that the phrase "My heart grew sick" (line 221) indicates that Montresor feels some remorse or hesitation; others may point to the fact that he makes no attempt to reverse his plan as evidence that he believes he has done the right thing.

ASSESSMENT PRACTICE I: *p. 80*	
1. A	5. B
2. D	6. D
3. C	7. B
4. C	8. C
Point out to students that the test-taking strategies they learned as they read can be used with the following item: • Item 7: multiple-meaning words (page 77)	

SHORT RESPONSE: DESCRIPTION Use this writing activity to determine whether students understand setting and can cite specific and relevant examples of imagery. Take them through the following steps:

- Have students analyze the prompt. They should notice that they will need to include specific examples of sensory images from the story.

- Tell them to review the parts of the story that describe the vault. They should list quotations from the story in the chart. Point out that they do not need to complete each row, but should include strong sensory details that give the reader a clear feeling of the setting.

- Remind students that they will use their own words to describe the setting and use the details from the chart to support their ideas.

TEST-TAKER'S TOOLKIT

Sight	The walls of the crypt are "lined with human remains . . . in the fashion of the great catacombs of Paris." The interior recess is "in depth about four feet, in width three, in height six or seven." Light gives off only "feeble rays."
Hearing	Fortunato: "a low moaning cry," "furious vibrations of the chain," "loud and shrill screams," at end, "only a jingling of the bells."
Smell	"the foulness of the air"
Taste	
Touch	The walls are "very damp," the granite walls feel very "solid."

SAMPLE DESCRIPTION

Fortunato meets his fate in a small crypt in the vast vaults below Montresor's estate. The setting is nearly dark—torches give off only "feeble rays," and the characters note "the foulness of the air" and the damp surfaces. The walls of this creepy, sinister place are "lined with human remains . . . in the fashion of the great catacombs of Paris." The setting is made complete with the details that the reader hears, such as Fortunato's "low moaning cry," his "furious vibrations of the chain," and his "loud and shrill screams." The last sensory detail the reader hears is the chilling description, "only a jingling of the bells."

SETTING A PURPOSE Complete the prereading activity on page 82 and review the teaching options below. Then share with your students what their goals will be, and use these goals to set a purpose for reading. Once students are clear on that purpose, have them write a purpose statement at the top of page 83.

TEST PREPARATION Direct students to read the multiple-choice questions on page 86, as well as the writing prompt on page 87, to help them focus their reading.

LEVEL 1

- **Where Corpses End Up**
- **Guerilla Literature: Plotting the Horror Short Story**

FOCUS SKILL: TRACE THE FLOW OF IDEAS

ACTIVITY: SURVEY IT

Have students complete the survey on page 82 about their preferences regarding horror stories. Students should share and discuss their responses with a partner or a small group.

OPTIONS FOR TEACHING

SKILL INSTRUCTION Use "Learn the Skill" at the bottom of page 82 and page R2 in the Nonfiction Skills Handbook to review the focus skill of tracing the flow of ideas.

> **ADDITIONAL RESOURCE:**
> **STANDARDS LESSON FILE:** READING AND INFORMATIONAL TEXTS: Recognizing Sequence and Chronological Order, page 53

JIGSAW LEARNING Divide the class into small groups, each responsible for learning and then sharing information about one of the following topics:
- Primal and other common fears
- Burial rituals

If you are using Level 2 in the same classroom, use "He Who Cast the First Stone Probably Didn't" as a resource.

BIBLIOGRAPHY Have students compile a list of classic horror stories and authors. Each student should contribute at least three entries. Create a classroom bibliography as a possible reading list.

LEVEL 2

- **He Who Cast the First Stone Probably Didn't**

FOCUS SKILL: TRACE THE FLOW OF IDEAS

ACTIVITY: DEBATE

Have students decide which twin's response is a more acceptable excuse, or whether neither is acceptable. Divide students into groups according to their responses and have them debate their opinions. After students have read the article, ask them to tell whether the article caused them to change their minds.

OPTIONS FOR TEACHING

SKILL INSTRUCTION Use "Learn the Skill" at the bottom of page 82 and page R2 in the Nonfiction Skills Handbook to review the focus skill of tracing the flow of ideas.

> **ADDITIONAL RESOURCE:**
> **STANDARDS LESSON FILE:** READING AND INFORMATIONAL TEXTS: Recognizing Sequence and Chronological Order, page 53

JIGSAW LEARNING Divide the class into small groups, each responsible for learning and then sharing information about one of the following topics:
- World conflicts in which revenge plays a key role
- Research on revenge and human behavior

If you are using Level 1 in the same classroom, add "Guerilla Literature: Plotting the Horror Short Story" to the list of resources.

INVESTIGATION Have students investigate game theory and games such as "Prisoner's Dilemma" and "Stag Hunt" that reveal human behavior. Have volunteers enact one or more of these games.

Where Corpses End Up

Flow of Ideas, page 83
Remind students that to scan, they look quickly over the lines in the text to find particular information. Students should circle *in order to* in lines 9–10, and *because* in line 14. Possible responses: bodies were covered in plaster, sealed in tombs, and perfume was burned; burial grounds were sacred under Roman law.

Make Inferences, page 83
Possible response: By including the quotation that tells how tourists reacted and responded on a visit to the catacombs, the reader gets a fuller picture of what the tombs are like. *Remediation Tip:* Have students cover the final paragraph and examine how the text becomes less powerful and interesting without the inclusion of the perspectives of the tourists.

Guerilla Literature: Plotting the Horror Short Story

Flow of Ideas, page 84
Students should check "you" (line 5, line 8); they should circle "Someone" (line 5), "everybody" and "They" (line 7), "she" (line 8), "Someone else" (line 11).

Possible response: Paying attention to the pronouns helps the reader understand who is involved in what happens. It also establishes that the narrator is a horror writer.

Visualize & Analyze, page 84
Students may underline the following:
• a hush over the forest (line 1)
• shining flashlights on their faces (line 2)
• The fire's crackling (line 3)
• A burning log pops . . . An owl hoots (lines 10–11)
• off among the skeleton trees (line 14)
Possible response: The author wants to create a setting that is similar to a horror story.

✓TestSmart page 85
Answer: B, "rules of combat"; Point out that students can locate the antecedent, *rules of combat*, in line 27 to confirm their answer choice.

Specialized Vocabulary, page 85
Students should underline "discover or develop in childhood" (line 39), and "of the dark, of the bogeyman . . . being killed" (lines 39–40). Possible response: basic fears, formed early in life

Clarify, page 85
Students should check *because a good horror story needs a good plot*. If they mark the other answer choice, ask them to offer support for that response.

ASSESSMENT PRACTICE II: *p. 86*	
1. D	5. A
2. D	6. B
3. B	7. C
4. A	8. C

He Who Cast the First Stone Probably Didn't

Flow of Ideas, page 83
Students will most likely circle "In virtually every human society" (lines 25–26). If other phrases are circled, ask students to explain their reasoning. The author's use of a personal anecdote helps readers connect the idea of revenge to a scenario that is likely to be familiar.

Specialized Vocabulary, page 83
Possible response: The prefix *re-* in the words *retaliation, retribution,* and *revenge* shows that the action implied in each word is a response to a previous action.

✓TestSmart page 84
Answer: C, "people remember the causes of their own words . . ." Point out that this article cites a number of research studies, so it is especially important to reread the appropriate section when a test question refers to a specific study.

Synthesize, page 85
Students should underline each of the two sentences in lines 186–194. Possible summary statements: We think of and perceive our own reasons and pain as the most important. These perceptions make people feel justified in continuing to hurt one another and unknowingly causes esculation.

Flow of Ideas, page 85
Possible response: The family story encourages the reader to use prior knowledge and experiences to better understand the information presented in the article. The anecdote at the beginning gives readers a framework to comprehend the article, and the reference at the end reminds readers that all retribution starts at a personal level.

ASSESSMENT PRACTICE II: *p. 86*	
1. D	5. B
2. A	6. A
3. D	7. B
4. C	8. A

LEVEL 1

Guide students through the steps described below under Guided Instruction. You may also wish to go over the rubric on the next page. (Consider modifying the rubric for these students, focusing only on Ideas, Organization, and Conventions.) Give students the entire 45 minutes to draft and review their responses. Point out, however, that in an actual timed writing situation, all steps of the writing process must be completed within the given time frame.

LEVEL 2

Share with students the rubric on the next page. Direct them to complete the entire writing process independently, within the actual 45-minute time frame they have been given.

GUIDED INSTRUCTION

ANALYZE THE PROMPT If necessary, lead the students through the two-step analysis process on page 87. Explain that low scores are often the result of the writer missing a critical piece of the directions. The marked prompt should look like this:

> How does Edgar Allan Poe use setting, imagery, and mood to play on his readers' primal fears in "The Cask of Amontillado"? Write an essay in which you identify three primal fears Poe exploits in his story and explain how he uses setting, imagery, and mood to conjure up those fears. Include specific details from the story to support your ideas.

- As needed, help students understand that a **primal fear** is a basic fear that many people share. Brainstorm examples of primal fears, such as a fear of heights or of the dark. During this discussion, students may identify some of these as fears used in Poe's story.
- Discuss each key element and explain how each will help to answer the question.

Have students jot down the circled words and phrases in the list of key elements. Remind them that all must be addressed in their response if they want to achieve the highest score on the test.

PLAN YOUR RESPONSE

- Review with students the steps of a timed writing assignment. For a prompt like this, which requires them to find evidence, remind them to budget enough time to find examples from the story. (They should probably spend no more than 10 to 15 minutes identifying their examples.)
- Students should identify and list three primal fears Poe uses in the story and write them in the chart. They should then review the story and find details of setting, imagery, and mood that illustrate each fear, and write these down in the chart. Remind students to use quotation marks around instances of exact words that Poe uses.

WRITE AND REVIEW Work together to brainstorm ideas for a conclusion. Encourage students to use their own words to create an original conclusion. When they have completed their draft, allow peers to comment on how well the students have met the requirements of the prompt.

RUBRIC FOR TIMED WRITING*

KEY TRAITS	3 (STRONG)	2 (AVERAGE)	1 (WEAK)
IDEAS	• The thesis statement is clear, focused, and compelling. • The analysis is insightful and reveals a deep understanding of the literary work. • Relevant details, examples, and quotations from the work support each key idea.	• The thesis statement is too broad or too narrow. • The analysis shows an adequate understanding of the literary work. • Most key ideas are supported by details, examples, and quotations from the work.	• The thesis statement is unclear or missing. • The analysis consists mostly of a plot summary. • Details, examples, and quotations from the work are not relevant or too scarce to support the key ideas.
ORGANIZATION	• The introduction is engaging and clearly presents the literary work to be discussed. • The conclusion summarizes the ideas and draws a conclusion or offers an observation. • Transitional words and phrases clearly show how ideas connect. • The organization is logical and follows essay form.	• The introduction presents the literary work, but it does not engage the reader. • The conclusion summarizes the ideas but only restates what has been said. • Most of the transitions work, but a few more are needed. • The organization shows some logic but does not follow a consistent pattern.	• The introduction does not clearly set up what the essay is about. • The essay lacks an identifiable conclusion. • The writer uses few, if any, transitional words. • The organization feels random or disjointed; the reader often feels lost or confused.
VOICE	• The tone and voice are appropriate for the purpose and audience. • The writing reflects active engagement with the literary work.	• The tone and voice are acceptable for the purpose and audience. • The writing lacks consistent engagement with the literary work.	• The voice lacks individuality and is not concerned with or not matched to the audience. • The writing is lifeless or mechanical.
WORD CHOICE	• Words are specific, accurate, and convey precise meaning. • Words and phrases convey an insightful understanding of the literary work.	• Words are adequate and mostly correct. • Familiar words and phrases communicate but rarely convey insights.	• Limited vocabulary and/or frequent misuse of parts of speech impair understanding. • Vague words limit the meaning conveyed.
SENTENCE FLUENCY	• Sentences vary in length and structure. • Sentence beginnings are varied.	• Sentences do not significantly vary in structure. • Some variety of sentence beginnings is attempted.	• Fragments and run-on sentences are frequent. • Many sentences begin the same way.
CONVENTIONS	• Spelling, capitalization, and punctuation are generally correct. • Grammar and usage are correct. • Paragraphing tends to be correct and reinforces the organization.	• Spelling, capitalization, and punctuation are sometimes uneven. • Grammar and usage do not distort meaning but are not always correct. • Paragraphing is attempted but is not always sound.	• Spelling, capitalization, and punctuation are frequently incorrect. • Grammar and usage mistakes are frequent and distort meaning. • Paragraphing is missing, irregular, or too frequent.

*Use the Literary Analysis Rubric on the WriteSmart CD if you wish to further modify this chart.

The Scarlet Ibis
by James Hurst

SUMMARY:

The narrator of "The Scarlet Ibis" recounts major events in the short life of Doodle, his disabled younger brother. To avoid being embarrassed by Doodle, he teaches Doodle to walk, but while he is leading him—sometimes heartlessly so—to further his accomplishments, Doodle dies in a thunderstorm.

RELATED NONFICTION:

LEVEL 1

MAGAZINE ARTICLE: "The Sibling Saga"
This magazine article talks about why siblings fight and offers tips for living with it. (*Readability*: Average)

MAGAZINE ARTICLE: "We Won the Lottery"
In this first-person essay, a young author discusses life with a brother who has special needs. (*Readability*: Easy)

LEVEL 2

BOOK EXCERPT: from *Special Siblings*
The emotional impact of having siblings with special needs is the subject of this excerpt. (*Readability*: Average)

MAGAZINE ARTICLE: "The Ties That Bind"
This magazine article is an interview with Francine Klagsbrun, author of a book about sibling relationships. (*Readability*: Challenging)

FOCUS AND MOTIVATE *p. 89*

FOR ALL STUDENTS

EXPLORE THE BIG QUESTION: *"Why do we HURT the ones we LOVE?"*
Discuss the question with students, asking them to consider family members or friends with whom they have a close relationship. Elicit or point out that cruelty may intrude on even the most loving relationships, leading to mixed emotions. Then have them complete the **Discuss** activity, allowing time for each group to share their ideas with the class.

INTRODUCE THE LESSON Tell students that in these selections, they will explore sibling rivalry and the mixed emotions that come with it. Students in Level 1 will read an article about why siblings fight and an essay by an author who has a brother with special needs. Students in Level 2 will read a book excerpt about the emotions involved in dealing with siblings who have special needs, plus an interview with the author of a book about the importance of sibling relationships. Call students' attention to the Assessment Goals at the bottom of the page.

ASSESSMENT GOALS

LEVEL 1

- analyze theme and symbol in fiction
- use active reading strategies to comprehend text
- identify the treatment and scope of nonfiction text
- analyze a writing prompt and plan an expository essay

LEVEL 2

- analyze theme and symbol in fiction
- apply critical thinking skills to analyze text
- analyze the treatment and scope of nonfiction text
- analyze a writing prompt and plan an expository essay

LEVEL 1

To discuss **symbol** and **theme**, use a familiar story. The following discussion uses the well-known story "Little Red Riding Hood."

SYMBOL: Some details of a story are the same, regardless of the narrator. For example, Little Red Riding Hood always meets a wolf in the woods while taking food to her grandmother; she also always strays from the intended path. Red Riding Hood is a symbol of youth going astray, and the wolf is a symbol of danger.

THEME: "Little Red Riding Hood" has several themes: children shouldn't talk to strangers; it is important to not stray from your task. Students can use the chart at the bottom of page 90 to explore other possible themes.

LEVEL 2

If helpful, review the concepts of symbol and theme. You may wish to include these additional points:

FOR SYMBOL

- A symbol can have more than one meaning: one very obvious, one deeper.
- An author might intend for readers to determine the meaning of a symbol for themselves. In other words, the meaning is not always exactly clear.
- Types of symbols include personal, cultural, and universal symbols.
- The word *sign* can be used for *symbol*. When discussing symbols, we use terms like "represents," "stands for," "expresses," and "suggests."

FOR THEME

- A theme can also be called a moral, a main idea, or a lesson.
- Repeated symbols are often a clue to the theme.
- Theme and subject are not the same. A theme gives a truth about a subject.

ADDITIONAL TERMS FOR CRITICAL ANALYSIS

To reinforce understanding of **atmosphere,** ask students to consider a scary movie. How does a director create a sense of fear and dread? The movie may feature a spooky, isolated house, shadowy scenes, and shrill violins for music. Include these points in your discussion:

- Atmosphere can help the reader determine the tone of a story.
- Atmosphere gives readers a sense of the author's feelings about the subject.
- Other factors that help create a particular atmosphere include colors, characters' body language, and certain prominent objects.

Tell students that many modern movies and television shows make **allusions** to classic literature. Include these points in your discussion:

- Many allusions come from Shakespeare plays and sonnets, the Bible, and Greek myths.
- Often, understanding the allusion is not necessary to understanding a story, but it does give insight to a character or theme.

ADDITIONAL RESOURCES
from **McDougal Littell Literature**

STUDENT'S EDITION
Literary Analysis Workshop, "Theme and Symbol," p. 402
Additional selection questions, p. 443

STANDARDS LESSON FILE: LITERATURE
Lesson 12: Theme, p. 103
Lesson 31: Symbol and Symbolism, p. 295

RESOURCE MANAGER
Selection Summary, p. 71
Additional Selection Questions, p. 67
Ideas for Extension, p. 68
Vocabulary Study, p. 77
Vocabulary Practice, p. 78
Reading Check, p. 80
Question Support, p. 81
Selection Test A, p. 85
Selection Test B/C, p. 87

BEST PRACTICES TOOLKIT
Analysis Frame: Theme, pp. D32, D33

VOCABULARY IN CONTEXT Read aloud the context phrases below and show students how to use context clues to figure out meaning. Once students have offered their own suggestions, review the actual definitions.

SELECTION VOCABULARY

imminent *(adj.)*: about to occur (line 167)

infallibility *(n.)*: an inability to make errors (line 222)

doggedness *(n.)*: persistence; stubbornness (line 277)

reiterate *(v.)*: to repeat (line 289)

precariously *(adj.)*: insecurely; in a dangerous or unstable way (line 303)

exotic *(adj.)*: excitingly strange (line 318)

evanesce *(v.)*: to disappear; vanish (line 392)

heresy *(n.)*: an action or opinion contrary to what is generally thought of as right (line 411)

CONTEXT PHRASES

1. chest pain signaling **imminent** danger of another heart attack

2. doubts about the coach's **infallibility** after the stunning defeat

3. **doggedness** in training for the skating competition six hours every day

4. didn't need to **reiterate** the story his mother had told a hundred times before

5. saw the plates stacked **precariously** seconds before they crashed

6. **exotic** flavors that made her want to visit the island just for the food

7. a betrayal that caused the public's trust in him to **evanesce**

8. dangerous beliefs that bordered on **heresy**

Make sure students are familiar with the following terms and references that appear in this story.

Idioms Review and discuss the following expressions with students.

- **be all there** (line 37): be capable of normal mental functioning
- **might turn out to be** (line 67): someday might become
- **if I so much** (line 76): if I even
- **when the going got rough** (line 86): when challenges arose
- **he was a sight** (line 88): he looked ridiculous
- **I was licked** (line 88): I was beaten
- **set out to** (line 127): attempted to

- **barring rain** (line 168): if it didn't rain
- **mooned around** (line 173): daydreamed or acted as if lost in a daydream
- **cross their hearts and hope to die** (lines 179–180): make a gesture that signifies a promise
- **don't you dare** (line 333): do not do what you are thinking about doing
- **there's no telling** (line 333): there is no way to predict or explain

Cultural References Guide students to use context clues to better understand the following references.

- **President Wilson** (line 19): Woodrow Wilson was president of the United States from 1913 to 1921.
- **left no crumbs behind** (line 278): a reference to the tale of Hansel and Gretel, who enter the forest and leave bread crumbs behind to find their way back home

- **"Shall We Gather at the River"** (line 339): a common funeral hymn that refers to the river of life running from the throne of God and the place where saints gather

The Scarlet Ibis

CLOSE READ

If you are using this selection primarily for **test preparation,** direct students to preview the multiple choice questions on page 103 and the writing prompt on page 104 to help focus their reading. Explain that this technique may be used any time they take a reading test.

Monitor, page 92

Students may underline:
- thought he was going to die (lines 22–23)
- build a little mahogany coffin for him (lines 25–26)
- might as well name him (line 27)

Students may suggest that Doodle defies expectations. Even though he is extremely frail, he surprises his family by living.

Make Inferences, page 92

Students should check *physically weak* and *determined.* *Remediation tip:* If students do not check *physically weak*, ask them why Doodle had such great difficulty trying to crawl, and why the doctor said the strain would probably kill him.

Pause & Reflect, page 93

INTERPRET Students should check *He resents being responsible for Doodle. Remediation tip:* If students choose "He enjoys having a constant companion," ask them what kinds of things they "lug" around. Are these pleasant things that they don't mind carrying with them?

Clarify, page 94

Students should underline:
- Doodle and I often went (line 99)
- we'd weave them (line 101)
- We'd bedeck ourselves (line 102)
- beyond the touch of the everyday world (line 103)
- we'd drop our jewels (lines 104–105)

You might want to point out that the narrator uses the word "we" to refer to himself and Doodle together only once earlier in the story. In this paragraph, "we" is used three times, as well as "Doodle and I" once. The language suggests the connection the narrator feels to his brother.

Monitor, page 94

We can be cruel to those we love, just as the human body can carry destructive germs or viruses that cause it to turn on itself.

Predict, page 94

Accept any well-supported response. Students who believe that the narrator will not be cruel to Doodle again may say that the narrator carries Doodle down the ladder after the coffin incident, which shows that he cares for his brother. Students who believe that the narrator will be cruel to Doodle again may say that he had to carry Doodle down the ladder anyway, and that he expresses no remorse for his actions.

Pause & Reflect, page 95

1. MONITOR Students should check *pride.* They should underline:
   - But all of us must have something or someone to be proud of, and Doodle had become mine. (lines 149–150)
   - I did not know then that pride is a wonderful, terrible thing, a seed that bears two vines, life and death. (lines 150–151)
2. *MAKE INFERENCES* Doodle's outlook changes from discouraged to hopeful. After weeks of trying to stand, he is able to stand on his own for a few moments. He thinks his brother will be proud of him for walking, so he keeps trying. *Remediation tip:* If students focus on Doodle's desire to walk without mentioning his brother's role, ask what effect the narrator's pride at Doodle's success (hugging, laughing, crying "yes, yes") had on Doodle's motivation for learning to walk.

✓TestSmart page 96

Answer: B, "taught Doodle to walk for selfish reasons"; Students should underline "taught him to walk" (line 188).

Pause & Reflect, page 97

1. *MAKE INFERENCES* Students should underline "run, to swim, to climb trees, and to fight" (line 224). As he did when he taught Doodle to walk, the narrator wants to surprise his parents with Doodle's new skills in order to feel the same sense of pride from them. He may also fear that they will disapprove.
2. INTERPRET Students should check a *new beginning.* *Remediation tip:* If students answer "warm weather," point out that symbolism is often reinforced with descriptive words and phrases. Ask students to underline words and phrases that hint at how the narrator and Doodle viewed the spring and summer. Students may note the following examples:
   - like a pot of gold (line 230)
   - Promise hung about us like the leaves (line 235)
   - ferns unfurled and birds broke into song (lines 235–236)

✓TestSmart Vocabulary, page 98

Answer: A, "to pass over without contact"

Make Inferences, page 98

The strain of doubling his efforts to do all that his brother wants him to do is too much for Doodle, and he is getting sick.

Visualize, page 99

Students might underline any of the following:
- hazy glare of the sun . . . still leaves (lines 300–301)
- bird the size of a chicken, with scarlet feathers and long legs (line 302)
- wings hung down loosely (line 303)
- feather dropped away and floated slowly down (lines 303–304)
- spray of flying feathers (line 311)
- it tumbled down . . . landing at our feet with a thud (lines 312–313)
- long, graceful neck jerked twice into an S (lines 313–314)
- white veil . . . the long white beak unhinged (lines 314–315)
- legs were crossed . . . clawlike feet were delicately curved (lines 315–316)
- like a broken vase of red flowers (line 317)

Students may answer that:

An unexpected event occurs when a strange red bird appears, and then dies, in the yard.

The bird may be a symbol for Doodle because, like him, the bird is beautiful but delicate.

Pause & Reflect, page 100
COMPARE Student responses should include
- the family's observations that both Doodle and the bird seem tired and sick
- that he and the ibis move in an uncoordinated, awkward manner
- the bird has long legs, and the narrator mentions Doodle's thin legs.

Students may point out that since Doodle's birth, the narrator has used the color red to describe Doodle (lines 22, 51, and 264) after an episode of physical exertion. They may also note that Doodle seems misplaced among his family members, as if he is from some other place, much as the ibis is not in its natural habitat.

Clarify, page 101
The narrator continues to run to punish Doodle for failing. Students should underline "The knowledge . . . that streak of cruelty within me awakened." (lines 386–387) *Remediation Tip:* Ask students to look for clues in the two preceding paragraphs that hint at the narrator's attitude toward Doodle by the time he begins to run. Students might underline:
- He had failed and we both knew it (lines 375–376)
- watching for a sign of mercy (line 378)
- he kept stepping on my heels (line 379)

Pause & Reflect, page 102
DRAW CONCLUSIONS The narrator calls Doodle his fallen scarlet ibis because, like Doodle, the ibis's journey through life took him further than anyone had expected, but the journey killed him. The author may be suggesting that pride can have damaging consequences, or that cruelty can make victims out of loved ones.

Big Question page 102
Accept any well-supported answer. Students may suggest that the narrator would respond that pride, jealousy, disappointment, and shame are felt more deeply when someone we love is involved. Such strong emotions may cause a person to lash out.

ASSESSMENT PRACTICE I: *p. 103*	
1. A	5. A
2. C	6. C
3. B	7. B
4. C	8. A

Point out to students that the test-taking strategies they learned as they read can be used with the following items:
- Item 4: matching words (page 96)
- Item 8: multiple-meaning words (page 98)

The Scarlet Ibis

SECOND READ: CRITICAL ANALYSIS

If you are using this selection primarily for **test preparation,** direct students to preview the multiple choice questions on page 103 and the writing prompt on page 104 to help focus their reading. Explain that this technique may be used any time they take a reading test.

Interpret, page 91
Students might identify any of the following symbols and interpretations:
- clove of seasons (line 1); the end of a period in the narrator's life
- bleeding tree (line 2); a memorial, something dying
- flower garden was stained (lines 2–3); something beautiful was ruined
- untenanted oriole nest (line 5); children are gone
- empty cradle (line 6); child has died
- graveyard flowers (line 6); flowers for the dead
- grindstone (lines 10 and 15); things become sharp and deadly

Interpret, page 92
The author includes details about the family's reaction to Doodle that are filled with imagery of Doodle's coming death. Students may underline:
- shriveled like an old man's (line 22)
- Everybody thought he was going to die (lines 22–23)
- build a little mahogany coffin for him (lines 25–26)
- Such a name sounds good only on a tombstone (line 29)

Analyze, page 92
Love can co-exist with cruelty, especially when joyful expectation turns to bitter disappointment.

Make Inferences, page 93
The nickname "Doodle" suggests that the family believed that the boy had little chance of amounting to anything, the way absent-minded doodling on paper is rarely anything except a waste of time. Students may underline:
- as if he were in reverse and couldn't change gears (lines 61–62)
- nobody expects much from someone called Doodle (line 69)

TestSmart Vocabulary, page 93
Answer: B, "defeated"

Compare, page 94
In the first boxed paragraph, the atmosphere is warm and peaceful; there is a sparkling, dreamlike quality. Students may underline:
- wildflowers, wild violets . . . and water lilies (lines 100–101)
- slanted rays of the sun burned orange (line 104)
- drop our jewels into the stream (line 105)

The next paragraph is colder and analytical, with few sensory descriptions except for those related to death. Students may underline:
- seed of our destruction (line 108)
- casket . . . Paris green sprinkled to kill the rats (lines 109–111)

Monitor, page 94
People can be especially cruel to those they love, in the same way our genetic makeup can be flawed by an inherited disease.

Analyze, page 95
Pride can be a source of great motivation, or it can lead to destructive actions.

✔**TestSmart** page 96
Answer: B, "taught Doodle to walk for selfish reasons"; Students should underline "taught him to walk" (line 188).

Interpret, page 97
Spring: optimism, hope for a new beginning; Summer: a time of labor, at the end of which is a reward or harvest. Symbolism is often reinforced with descriptive words and phrases. As needed, ask students to underline similes and imagery that hint at how the narrator and Doodle viewed the spring and summer.
- Success . . . like a pot of gold (lines 229–230)
- Promise . . . like the leaves (line 235)
- wherever we looked, ferns unfurled and birds broke into song (lines 235–236)

✔**TestSmart** page 98
Answer: A, "foreboding"; Students may underline:
- there was no rain and the crops withered, curled up, then died (line 238)
- hurricane came out of the east (line 239)
- the ruin (line 247)

Analyze, page 98
Students' prior knowledge of World War I may vary. Accept all well-reasoned answers. Many students will note that although wars may be fought for noble reasons, they inevitably lead to death and destruction. Students who have studied World War I should recognize that it began as an act of pride and anger (Austria-Hungary's retaliation against Serbia for the assassination of Archduke Franz Ferdinand) among "brothers" (humans). This is like the narrator's campaign to improve Doodle, which was also initiated by pride. Like Doodle's life, the war ended tragically with the deaths of many soldiers and civilians.

Compare, page 99
Students should point out that:
- both the bird and Doodle fall awkwardly or into an awkward position
- Doodle's neck and chest are red with blood like the red feathers of the bird
- both have slender necks
- Doodle's thin legs, bending "sharply at the knees" would appear birdlike

Like Doodle, the ibis arrived with almost no chance of surviving long in that environment. Delicate and awkward, Doodle is also like the ibis in that his journey through life took him further than anyone had expected.

Compare, page 100
Students should underline:
- He took out a piece of string . . . looped one end around its neck (lines 337–339)
- singing softly "Shall We Gather at the River" (line 339)

- carried the bird . . . dug a hole in the flower garden (lines 340–341)
Students should double-underline:
- Daddy, Mama, and I went back . . . watched Doodle through the open door (lines 336–337)
- we were watching him through the front window (lines 341–342)
- made us laugh (line 343)
- we covered our mouths with our hands (line 344)
His family seems to view Doodle as a ridiculous, comic character whose actions are childlike and silly rather than serious and heartfelt. They do not recognize his connection to, and respect for, the death of another creature.

Compare, page 101
In both incidents, Doodle does something he isn't personally motivated to do in order to please his brother. Doodle cries, "Brother, Brother, don't leave me!" which seems to fuel the narrator's cruelty.

Evaluate, page 102
Accept any well-reasoned response. Students should consider details from the story that support their positions. Those claiming that the relationship between the narrator and Doodle is realistic might point out that
- siblings can be cruel to each other
- younger brothers will often look up to their older brothers and want to follow them around
- in a rural community Doodle may have been the narrator's only close playmate, forcing him to spend a great deal of time with a boy who disappointed him
Those who believe that the relationship between the narrator and Doodle is not realistic might point out that
- the narrator casts himself as Doodle's only real caretaker, which is unlikely given that Doodle has special needs
- a preteen boy would probably not take it upon himself to spend his summer teaching his brother to walk, even if it could be done

Big Question page 102
The narrator's pride and disappointment cause him to suppress his love for his brother, allowing him to act on his worst impulses. The evidence that the narrator's grief is genuine begins in lines 106–107 when the narrator states, "There is within me . . . a knot of cruelty." This suggests that, from the moment he makes the "tear-blurred" connection between the ibis and Doodle in line 407 to the time this story is written, the narrator's feeling that he has caused Doodle's death has haunted him.

ASSESSMENT PRACTICE I: *p. 103*	
1. D	5. A
2. C	6. C
3. C	7. B
4. A	8. A

Point out to students that the test-taking strategies they learned as they read can be used with the following items:
- Item 3: matching words (page 96)
- Item 4: evaluate atmosphere (page 98)
- Item 8: multiple-meaning words (page 93)

SHORT RESPONSE: EVALUATE SYMBOLISM Use this writing activity to determine whether students understand symbolism. Take them through the following steps:

- Have students analyze the prompt. They should notice that they are being asked to write about things that are symbols for Doodle or his death.
- Tell them to complete the chart, listing the two symbols they have chosen and related details from the text.
- Lastly, tell students to write a response that includes a description of the symbols, supporting details from the text, and an explanation of the meaning of the symbols.

TEST-TAKER'S TOOLKIT

SYMBOL	SUPPORT FROM THE TEXT
the scarlet ibis	"It looks tired … maybe sick." (line 306)
	"long, graceful neck" (line 313); Doodle's neck: "unusually long and slim" (line 405).
	"A white veil" (line 314) like Doodle's caul at birth
Doodle's nickname	"Mama and Daddy thought it was a better name" (line 65)
	"nobody expects much from someone called Doodle" (line 69)

SAMPLE EVALUATION

Two symbols for Doodle in "The Scarlet Ibis" are his nickname and the scarlet ibis. The narrator's statement that "nobody expects much from someone called Doodle" symbolizes the family's attitude toward Doodle as a baby. The fact that Doodle's parents approved of the nickname indicates that they didn't believe their son deserved a "strong" name like William Armstrong.

The scarlet ibis is a symbol for Doodle. Like Doodle, it "looks tired … maybe sick." The white veil that comes over the ibis's eyes in death is reminiscent of Doodle's caul at birth. The two also look alike when they die. For example, the bird has a "long, graceful neck" and Doodle's neck is described as "unusually long and slim." Their legs, position, and color are similar. Like Doodle, the ibis is far away from its natural habitat, and both are fragile in their environment.

SETTING A PURPOSE Complete the prereading activity on page 105 and review the teaching options below. Then share with your students what their goals will be, and use these goals to set a purpose for reading. Once students are clear on that purpose, have them write a purpose statement at the top of page 106.

TEST PREPARATION Direct students to read the multiple-choice questions on page 112, as well as the writing prompt on page 113, to help them focus their reading.

<table>
<tr><td>

LEVEL 1

- **The Sibling Saga**
- **We Won the Lottery**

FOCUS SKILL: IDENTIFY TREATMENT AND SCOPE

ACTIVITY: ANTICIPATION/REACTION GUIDE

Before assigning the related readings, introduce the Anticipation/Reaction Guide and have students complete it individually and then discuss it in pairs. After students have read the articles, ask them to revisit the guide to respond again to the statements. Have them discuss which responses changed, if any, and why.

OPTIONS FOR TEACHING

SKILL INSTRUCTION Use "Learn the Skill" at the bottom of page 105 and page R2 in the Nonfiction Skills Handbook to review the focus skill of identifying treatment and scope.

> **ADDITIONAL RESOURCES:**
> **STANDARDS LESSON FILE: READING AND INFORMATION TEXTS:** Drawing Conclusions, page 81

JIGSAW LEARNING Divide the class into small groups, each responsible for one of these topics:
- causes of sibling rivalry
- responsibilities of those with disabled siblings

To accommodate Level 2 students, add a third topic about birth influences and add "The Ties That Bind" as a resource.

INTERVIEW Have classmates interview each other about their relationships with siblings. Do they get along? Do their parents/guardians give each the same attention? Have only children talk about whether they ever wished they had siblings.

</td><td>

LEVEL 2

- **from *Special Siblings***
- **The Ties That Bind**

FOCUS SKILL: ANALYZE TREATMENT AND SCOPE

ACTIVITY: CHART IT

Before assigning the related readings, introduce the cause-effect chart and have partners work together to identify *Sibling's Words or Actions* as well as possible effects. After they have read the selections, ask partners to discuss whether they would make any changes to their cause-effect chart as a result of what they have learned.

OPTIONS FOR TEACHING

SKILL INSTRUCTION Use "Learn the Skill" at the bottom of page 105 and page R2 in the Nonfiction Skills Handbook to review the focus skill of analyzing treatment and scope.

> **ADDITIONAL RESOURCES:**
> **STANDARDS LESSON FILE: READING AND INFORMATION TEXTS:** Drawing Conclusions, page 91

JIGSAW LEARNING Divide the class into small groups, each responsible for one of the following topics:
- support groups/organizations for siblings of children with special needs
- relationships among same and different genders of siblings

To accomodate Level 1, add a topic about how to cope with problems in sibling relationships and add "The Sibling Saga" to the list of resources.

DISCUSS Use "The Ties That Bind" as a basis for a discussion about the importance of both sibling-sibling and parent-child relationships in childhood.

</td></tr>
</table>

The Sibling Saga

Treatment & Scope, page 106
Students should underline "sibling rivalry" (line 13).

Treatment & Scope, page 107
Students should check *informational article*.

✓**TestSmart** page 107

Answer: A, "healthy in the right amount"; Students should underline clues such as "Sibling rivalry can be a positive thing" (line 32) and "Healthful competition" (line 37).

Treatment & Scope, page 108
Students should check *informative*. The author mostly presents research and facts rather than emotions. The anecdotes are not dramatic or funny, but they support the expert information about the causes of, and responses to, sibling rivalry.

Treatment & Scope, page 108
The article discusses biological causes of sibling rivalry, plus its pros and cons. The article also provides suggestions on how to deal with sibling rivalry.

We Won the Lottery

Treatment & Scope, page 109
Students should check *personal essay. Remediation Tip:* Students who need help distinguishing a letter from a personal essay could be asked to consider that, while both would be written in the first person, the essay has no stated audience and lacks features of correspondence such as a salutation and closing.

Treatment & Scope, page 110
Students should check *to inform*. The author's main idea, the last sentence of the essay on lines 181–185, explains what the author wants the reader to know about how his relationship with his brother affected his life, but he doesn't try to convince the reader to change his or her opinion or to take action. He describes life with his brother in a factual manner.

Evaluate, page 110
Student responses may vary. Students who believe that the parents did a good job may cite:
- they did not want to overload me (lines 36–37)
- only once . . . "outside of the circle" (lines 97–99)
- he knew that the situation was tough on me (lines 102–103)
- My mother called me every day . . . she spent a lot of extra time with me (lines 106–109)
- mother would have to drop subtle hints . . . paying attention to Mikey (lines 132–134)

Students who believe that the parents did not do a good job might say that they should have been more upfront about Mikey's condition early in his life (lines 20–29) and later, when he seemed to be getting worse and was headed for a difficult and dangerous surgery (lines 145–154). They may believe that the parents are too subtle in trying to help the author understand the situations.

Specialized Vocabulary, page 111
Students should underline:
- had to stay in the hospital (lines 160–161)
- didn't look like himself (lines 164–165)
- made a complete recovery (lines 167–168)

Definition: n. an acute or chronic disease marked by inflammation of the lungs and caused by viruses, bacteria, or other microorganisms and sometimes by physical and chemical irritants

✓**TestSmart** page 111

Answer: D, "one family's experience of living with a child with disabilities"
Students should underline:
- Introduction: brotherly bond is there (line 13)
- His Own Way: toughest and weakest kid I have ever known (lines 61–62)
- Important Lessons: taught me how to handle certain situations (lines 79–80)
- Reality Check: when I opened my eyes to what my parents had been trying to show me (lines 146–148)
- Complete Recovery: he made a complete recovery (lines 167–168)

ASSESSMENT PRACTICE II: *p. 112*	
1. D	5. C
2. B	6. B
3. B	7. A
4. A	8. D

Point out to students that the test-taking strategies they learned as they read can be used with the following item:
- Item 2: evaluate scope (page 111)

from *Special Siblings*

Treatment & Scope, page 106
The author focuses on the negative feelings that a child can experience growing up with a sibling with special needs. *Remediation Tip:* Suggest to students who need help identifying the treatment and scope that scanning the excerpt's subheadings can provide a rough outline of the content.

Treatment & Scope, page 107
The author is ashamed of the way she behaved toward her brother as a child. She may be writing to let other people in the same situation know that their feelings are normal.
Students may circle:
- When I think . . . I cringe at my cruelty (lines 43–44)
- I wasn't really that different from other big sisters (lines 44–45)
- the realization . . . doesn't do much for my self-esteem (lines 46–47)

✓TestSmart page 107
Answer: C, "regretful"; Students may underline:
- I took advantage of him and I really should not have. (lines 52–53)
- I'm lucky. I have the chance to include him in my life now. (lines 66–67)

Connect, page 108
Student responses will vary; accept any well-reasoned answer that relates either to embarrassment and conflict avoidance if students relate to the author, or to loyalty to family against outsiders if students connect with Gwen.

Treatment & Scope, page 108
This excerpt has a narrow scope because the author only talks about the negative emotions that a child may deal with when he or she has a special-needs sibling.

The Ties That Bind

Treatment & Scope, page 109
Students should check *informational interview.*

Treatment & Scope, page 110
"Again he had outdone me" conveys a tone of jealousy, competitiveness, and frustration that her brother always wins. As the interview continues, the author's tone becomes somewhat impersonal and academic.
Students might underline:
- Sigmund Freud . . . relationship with his parents (lines 26–27)
- one can be just as permanently influenced . . . by a sibling (lines 28–29)
- patterns established in childhood . . . destructive ways (lines 32–33)

✓TestSmart page 111
Answer: C, "siblings' influence within the family and in outside relationships."
Students should underline:
- Introduction: have an effect on our adult lives as profound as the parent-child relationship (lines 7–8)
- Did childhood rivalries . . . : If Robert was so significant in my life, this had to be true for others (lines 22–23)
- How do siblings . . . : patterns established in childhood then get replayed (lines 32–33)
- What about outside . . . : you would likely act the same (line 39)
- Do birth order . . . : certainly influences your identity, but it goes beyond just that (lines 45–46)
- How can we . . . : be aware that something is wrong (line 52); speak to your sibling (line 54); move on to reshaping how you behave with others (line 56)
- Why is it . . . : we need brothers and sisters to support us emotionally (lines 62–63)
- If society is . . . : reap all the rewards you can from bonds you do have (line 71)

ASSESSMENT PRACTICE II: *p. 112*	
1. A	5. D
2. C	6. B
3. D	7. C
4. B	8. A

Point out to students that the test-taking strategies they learned as they read can be used with the following item:
- Item 3: infertone (page 107)

LEVEL 1

Guide students through the steps described below under Guided Instruction. You may also wish to go over the rubric on the next page. (Consider modifying the rubric for these students, focusing only on Ideas, Organization, and Conventions.) Give students the entire 45 minutes to draft and review their responses. Point out, however, that in an actual timed writing situation, all steps of the writing process must be completed within the given time frame.

LEVEL 2

Share with students the rubric on the next page. Direct them to complete the entire writing process independently, within the actual 45-minute time frame they have been given.

GUIDED INSTRUCTION

ANALYZE THE PROMPT If necessary, lead the students through the four-step analysis process on page 113. Explain that low scores are often the result of the writer missing a critical piece of the directions. The marked prompt should look like this:

> Each of the selections you have read examines love and conflict in sibling relationships. Can conflict with siblings be avoided? Why or why not? Write an expository essay in which you explain whether it is possible to avoid sibling rivalry. Use details and examples from the readings to support your ideas.

- Remind students that an expository essay is an essay that gives information. The tone should be academic, and the use of the pronoun *I* should be limited or avoided.

- Suggest that students restate the prompt as something similar to "I am being asked to explain whether sibling rivalry can be avoided."

- Remind students that the underlined words and phrases should be addressed in their response if they want to achieve the highest score on the test.

PLAN YOUR RESPONSE

- Review with students the steps of a timed writing assignment. For a prompt like this, which requires the use of details and examples, remind them to budget enough time to find examples in the text.

- Students should jot down their answers and details and examples in the chart. Point out, however, that in a real testing situation they would have had to plan the organization of their own writing. Show them how the key words in the prompt suggest what the chart's labels should be.

WRITE AND REVIEW Encourage students to write two or three opening sentences based on the suggestions (using peer feedback to choose the best if time allows). When they have completed their draft, allow peers to comment on how well the students have met the requirements of the prompt.

RUBRIC FOR TIMED WRITING*

KEY TRAITS	3 (STRONG)	2 (AVERAGE)	1 (WEAK)
IDEAS	• The thesis statement is clear and focused and presents the topic discussed. • The key ideas are well supported by relevant details and examples. • The writer connects solid examples to defend the thesis in thoughtful ways. • The ideas are well thought out, original, and hold the reader's attention.	• The thesis statement is too broad or too narrow but loosely presents the subject of the essay. • Most details and examples are relevant in supporting key ideas. • The writer connects examples to defend the thesis in adequate ways. • The ideas are satisfactory and mostly hold the reader's attention.	• The thesis statement is unclear or missing; it does not identify the subject of the essay. • Details and examples are irrelevant or missing and do not support key ideas. • The writer does not connect examples to defend the thesis. • The ideas are repetitive or lack a clear point.
ORGANIZATION	• The introduction clearly presents the topic in an interesting, informative way. • The essay wraps up with a satisfying conclusion or offers an observation. • Transitional words and phrases clearly show how ideas connect. • The organization is logical and follows a consistent pattern.	• The introduction presents the topic, but it does not engage the reader. • The conclusion only restates what has been said. • Most of the transitions work, but a few more are needed. • The organization shows some logic but does not follow a consistent pattern.	• The introduction does not clearly set up what the essay is about. • The essay lacks an identifiable conclusion. • The writer uses few, if any, transitional words. • The organization feels random or disjointed; the reader often feels lost or confused.
VOICE	• The tone and voice are appropriate for the purpose and audience.	• The tone and voice are acceptable for the purpose and audience but not strongly individual or direct.	• The voice lacks individuality and is not concerned with or not matched to the audience.
WORD CHOICE	• Words are specific, accurate, and convey precise meaning.	• Words are adequate and mostly correct.	• Limited vocabulary and/or frequent misuse of parts of speech impair understanding.
SENTENCE FLUENCY	• Sentences vary in length and structure. • Sentence beginnings are varied.	• Sentences do not significantly vary in structure, and some fragments and run-on sentences are present. • Sentence beginnings are mostly the same.	• Repetitive sentence structure, fragments, and run-on sentences make the writing difficult to follow. • Most or all sentences begin the same way.
CONVENTIONS	• Spelling, capitalization, and punctuation are generally correct. • Grammar and usage are correct. • Paragraphing tends to be correct and reinforces the organization.	• Spelling, capitalization, and punctuation are sometimes uneven. • Grammar and usage do not distort meaning but are not always correct. • Paragraphing is attempted but is not always sound.	• Spelling, capitalization, and punctuation are frequently incorrect. • Grammar and usage mistakes are frequent and distort meaning. • Paragraphing is missing, irregular, or too frequent.

*Use the Informative Essay and Interview Rubric on the WriteSmart CD if you wish to further modify this chart.

The Lost Boys
by Sara Corbett

SUMMARY:

"The Lost Boys" describes the plight of orphaned African boys who fled Sudan during a hostile civil war. Sara Corbett's article presents the challenges faced by the roughly 10,000 survivors. It then focuses on the three Dut brothers, refugees who have been resettled in Fargo, North Dakota, and who are trying to adjust to their new life.

RELATED NONFICTION:

LEVEL 1

MAGAZINE ARTICLE: "The Lost Boys of Sudan"
This article outlines how thousands of Sudanese boys were forced to take dangerous journeys to escape war in their homeland and how some survivors came to find a new life in the United States. (*Readability*: Average)

MAGAZINE ARTICLE: "Kids on the Run"
This article takes a look at the impact of war on children around the world. (*Readability*: Easy)

LEVEL 2

NEWSPAPER INTERVIEW: "In a Strange Land, Trailed by Cameras"
The author of this article interviews John Bul Dau, a Lost Boy, and the filmmaker Christopher Quinn, who made a movie documenting the experiences of the Lost Boys. (*Readability*: Average)

MAGAZINE ARTICLE: "I Have Had to Learn to Live with Peace"
In this article, Alephonsion Deng movingly shares the challenges he has faced as a Lost Boy and examines the trials he continues to confront in his daily life in San Diego, California. (*Readability*: Average)

FOCUS AND MOTIVATE *p. 115*

FOR ALL STUDENTS

EXPLORE THE BIG QUESTION: *"How far would you go to find FREEDOM?"*
Have students suggest situations that could cause people to leave their country, such as civil war or religious persecution. Discuss the question with students, and guide them to understand that while it might be difficult to imagine these kinds of events in the United States, many people in the world today find that they have no choice but to leave their homelands. Then have them complete the **Chart It** activity. Encourage students to include details to describe at least one specific example in each category.

INTRODUCE THE LESSON Tell students that in these selections, they will learn about the complicated lives of the Lost Boys of Sudan. Then call their attention to the Assessment Goals at the bottom of the page.

ASSESSMENT GOALS

LEVEL 1

- identify the author's purpose in a work of nonfiction
- use active reading strategies to comprehend text
- synthesize information from nonfiction texts
- analyze a writing prompt and plan a problem-solution essay

LEVEL 2

- analyze the author's purpose in a work of nonfiction
- apply critical thinking skills to analyze text
- synthesize information from nonfiction texts
- analyze a writing prompt and plan a problem-solution essay

LEVEL 1

Tell students that you will read aloud some passages from texts about the same general topic. Explain that they should listen to determine the **author's purpose** in each. Then read aloud the following examples, one at a time. Have students identify the author's purpose and explain the clues that helped them arrive at their response.

Workers who make a habit of being late can cost their employers millions of dollars each day in lost productivity. Some businesses are considering plans to subtract wages or to charge a fee to address these losses. (to inform or explain)

Shelly sat up in bed with a start and glared at the clock on her nightstand. *That's just great,* she thought. *Now I'm an hour late for swimming practice.* (to entertain)

Giving young people alarm clocks is the first step in developing their sense of responsibility about being on time. It is time for parents to start teaching their children that the world will not wait for them to get going. (to persuade)

I truly enjoy hanging out in the morning, taking my time reading the papers. It wasn't until I got fired that I stopped to think about what that last, lingering cup of coffee might actually cost me. (to express thoughts or feelings)

LEVEL 2

As you discuss author's purpose, you may wish to include these additional points:

- Identifying a text's genre often helps uncover the author's purpose.
- Your reaction to a text, such as amusement, interest, or inspiration, can also provide a clue to the author's purpose.
- An author may have more than one purpose for writing.

ADDITIONAL TERMS FOR CRITICAL ANALYSIS

Include the following points about the use of **anecdotes:**

- Authors use anecdotes to make their ideas come to life for readers.
- Readers tend to remember important ideas if they are supported by vivid, memorable anecdotes.

ADDITIONAL RESOURCES
from McDougal Littell Literature

STUDENT'S EDITION

Critical Reading Workshop, "Author's Purpose," p. 508

Additional selection questions, p. 554

STANDARDS LESSON FILE: READING AND INFORMATIONAL TEXTS

Lesson 3: Determining Author's Purpose, p. 23

RESOURCE MANAGER

Selection Summary, pp. 99, 100

Additional Selection Questions, p. 95

Ideas for Extension, p. 96

Vocabulary Study, p. 105

Vocabulary Practice, p. 106

Reading Check, p. 109

Question Support, p. 111

Selection Test A, p. 113

Selection Test B/C, p. 115

BEST PRACTICES TOOLKIT

Informative Essay, p. C29

PRETEACH VOCABULARY

FOR ALL STUDENTS

VOCABULARY IN CONTEXT Read aloud the context phrases below and show students how to use context clues to figure out meaning. Once students have offered their own suggestions, review the actual definitions.

SELECTION VOCABULARY

fractious *(adj.)*: hard to manage or hold together; unruly (line 28)

posse *(n.)*: a band (line 31)

exodus *(n.)*: a mass departure (line 33)

marauding *(adj.)*: roaming about in search of plunder (line 41)

subsist *(v.)*: to support oneself at a minimal level (line 46)

boon *(n.)*: a benefit; blessing (line 91)

CONTEXT PHRASES

1. a **fractious** disagreement over ownership

2. a **posse** of travelers arriving at a hotel

3. making a rain-soaked **exodus** from the beach

4. **marauding** bandits terrorized the neighborhood

5. **subsist** only on vegetables from the garden

6. new jobs that are a **boon** to the local economy

FOR ENGLISH LEARNERS

Make sure students are familiar with the following terms and references that appear in this story.

Idioms Review and discuss the following expressions with students.

- **out of the question** (line 51): impossible
- **showing up** (line 75): arriving

Cultural References Review or discuss the following terms with students.

- **Islamic government** (lines 28–29): a country or nation that governs based on the teachings of the prophet Mohammed
- **Christianity** (line 29): religious beliefs based on the teachings of Jesus Christ
- **Peter Pan** (line 31): the title character in a children's fantasy story about a boy who refuses to grow up
- **foster homes** (line 52) families that temporarily take in children who do not have relatives to care for them
- **food stamps** (line 112) part of a U.S. government program that helps low-income people get food

The Lost Boys

CLOSE READ

If you are using this selection primarily for **test preparation,** direct students to preview the multiple choice questions on page 122 and the writing prompt on page 123 to help focus their reading. Explain that this technique may be used any time they take a reading test.

Monitor, page 118

Students should underline the sentence that explains who the Lost Boys are in lines 25–28. *Remediation Tip* Help students analyze the sentence. Point out that while line 25 begins by telling about Peter Dut and his brothers, as it continues, it explains who the Lost Boys are. Have students compare this information with the anecdote in the preceding paragraph.

Pause & Reflect, page 119

1. *SUMMARIZE* Thousands of Lost Boys traveled between Sudan, Ethiopia, and Kenya. A great number died along the way, from starvation, thirst, and attacks by wild animals. About half of the original number finally arrived at a refugee camp in Kenya.
2. *PREDICT* Accept all reasonable predictions. Responses will likely predict that the boys will encounter great differences in culture, technology, and climate.

Pause & Reflect, page 120

DRAW CONCLUSIONS Students should check *to entertain readers with a funny story*. Remind students that an author may have more than one purpose in writing. While the author's purpose for the article as a whole is to inform, the anecdote in lines 77–85 is meant to entertain. Point out the use of humorous images, such as "grins sheepishly" and "And so begins an opening spree."

TestSmart page 120

Answer: D, "will lose their African identity"; If necessary, point out that this answer appears directly in the text in lines 122–123.

Pause & Reflect, page 121

MAKE INFERENCES Students may underline "ignored by white students around him" (line 107), "trying not to look at the short skirts" (lines 109–110), "worries about money" (line 111). Students may suggest that for the first three months, almost everything is new to the boys. As time passes, they will become more familiar with American life and customs, and they will start to make friends.

Big Question page 121

Responses may include a range of ideas. Accept any well-supported answer. Some students may cite the myriad physical dangers the boys faced. Others may feel that the culture shock and separation from all they know was a greater challenge.

ASSESSMENT PRACTICE I: *p. 122*	
1. D	5. B
2. B	6. C
3. A	7. C
4. A	8. D

Point out to students that the test-taking strategies they learned as they read can be used with the following item:
• Item 2: identify a main reason (page 120)

The Lost Boys

SECOND READ: CRITICAL ANALYSIS

If you are using this selection primarily for **test preparation,** direct students to preview the multiple choice questions on page 122 and the writing prompt on page 123 to help focus their reading. Explain that this technique may be used any time they take a reading test.

Analyze, page 117

Students may indicate that the anecdote draws readers into the article; a presentation of facts might be less interesting to readers. Some may note that since the author wants readers to learn about the Lost Boys, she makes a choice to present them as individuals first, and then later brings in facts and statistics.

Analyze, page 118

Students might underline the following:

- roughly 10,000 boys . . . Kenya in 1992 (line 27)
- trekked about 1,000 miles . . . finally to Kenya (lines 35–36)
- majority of the boys belonged to the Dinka or Nuer tribes (lines 36–37)
- most were between the ages of 8 and 18 (lines 37–38)

Authors present facts when their purpose is to inform.

✓TestSmart Vocabulary, page 119

Answer: B, "forced to leave"; Remind students that they can also use context clues if they are still unsure of which answer choice is correct.

Evaluate, page 119

Students should underline the sentence in lines 59–60 in which the author describes her wait for the boys at the Fargo airport. Students may say that the change to first-person point of view is effective in that it allows readers to re-connect to the Duts' journey, after the presentation of factual background information in lines 25–57. The change is effective in supporting the author's purpose to inform, because it provides specific examples of the challenges the brothers are facing.

Analyze, page 120

Each anecdote reflects a different aspect of the problems the brothers face as they adjust to life in Fargo; they help the reader make a personal connection with these real people and their very real difficulties and challenges.

✓TestSmart page 120

Answer: D, "will lose their African identity"; If needed, point out that this answer appears directly in the text in lines 122–123.

Big Question page 121

Allow any well-supported answer. Responses may include ideas such as the following: These young men work to remember that while life in Fargo may be extremely challenging, they have freedoms that are not available to those in their homeland; most readers will note and appreciate that the idea of freedom is key to life in the United States.

ASSESSMENT PRACTICE I: *p. 122*	
1. D	5. B
2. C	6. C
3. A	7. C
4. A	8. D

Point out to students that the test-taking strategies they learned as they read can be used with the following item:
- Item 2: identify a main reason (page 120)

SHORT RESPONSE: PARAGRAPH Use this writing activity to determine whether students understand author's purpose and can cite specific examples that support their ideas. Take them through the following steps:

- Have students analyze the prompt. They should notice that they need to cite specific examples from the article.

- Have them review the article to complete the chart. Point out that they may not find evidence for each category. While some students may feel that they know the author's purpose is to inform or explain, completing the chart will help them be certain of their idea and will allow them to have a list of lines they may use as supporting evidence.

- Explain that if they find that they have many entries for one category, they might want to mark important entries with an asterisk to use in their paragraphs.

TEST-TAKER'S TOOLKIT

Author's Purpose in "The Lost Boys"			
To Persuade	**To Entertain**	**To Inform or Explain**	**To Express Thoughts and Feelings**
	lines 81–85	*lines 3–19, lines 25–39, lines 46–57, lines 59–65, lines 73–75, lines 94–99, lines 106–113, lines 122–126*	*lines 75–76, lines 128–136*

SAMPLE PARAGRAPH

While Sara Corbett has more than one purpose for writing "The Lost Boys," her main purpose is to inform readers about the plight of the Lost Boys of Sudan and to explain the complicated lives they have had and the challenges they still face. In lines 25–39, Corbett informs the reader about who the Lost Boys are and what happened to them in Sudan. She also explains how many of them have been arriving in the United States in lines 46–57. Corbett carefully includes a number of anecdotes about three Sudanese brothers and how they deal with their new lives in a very effective way, such as in lines 3–19, 59–65, and 106–113 that inform and touch the reader in a very personal way.

SETTING A PURPOSE Complete the prereading activity on page 124 and review the teaching options below. Then share with your students what their goals will be, and use these goals to set a purpose for reading. Once students are clear on that purpose, have them write a purpose statement at the top of page 125.

TEST PREPARATION Direct students to read the multiple-choice questions on page 130, as well as the writing prompt on page 131, to help them focus their reading.

<table>
<tr><td>

LEVEL 1

</td><td>

LEVEL 2

</td></tr>
<tr><td>

- ## The Lost Boys of Sudan

- ## Kids on the Run

FOCUS SKILL: SYNTHESIZE

ACTIVITY: CHART IT

Have students work with a partner to complete the chart on page 124 about traveling to another country without an adult.

OPTIONS FOR TEACHING

SKILL INSTRUCTION Use "Learn the Skill" at the bottom of page 124 and page R2 in the Nonfiction Skills Handbook to review the focus skill of synthesizing.

> **ADDITIONAL RESOURCES:**
>
> **STANDARDS LESSON FILE:** READING AND INFORMATIONAL TEXTS: Lesson 14: Synthesizing Information, page 133

DISCUSSION Divide the class into small groups. Have groups discuss all of the texts they have read, using the following questions to guide the discussion:

- Which aspects of the Lost Boys' lives do you think have been the most challenging?
- Which reading did you find most interesting? Why?
- What new insights did you gain about people who come to the United States from a war-torn country?

If you are using Level 2 in the same classroom, have mixed groups briefly describe and summarize the texts they have read before they begin their discussion.

INVESTIGATION Have students investigate relief organizations, such as the American Red Cross, that have worked to provide aid the Lost Boys and other Sudanese refugees and discuss their efforts.

</td><td>

- ## In a Strange Land, Trailed by Cameras

- ## I Have Had to Learn to Live with Peace

FOCUS SKILL: SYNTHESIZE

ACTIVITY: CONDUCT AN INTERVIEW

Before assigning the related nonfiction readings, have partners interview each other using the questions on page 124.

OPTIONS FOR TEACHING

SKILL INSTRUCTION Use "Learn the Skill" at the bottom of page 124 and page R2 in the Nonfiction Skills Handbook to review the focus skill of synthesizing.

> **ADDITIONAL RESOURCES:**
>
> **STANDARDS LESSON FILE:** READING AND INFORMATIONAL TEXTS: Lesson 14: Synthesizing Information, page 133

FILM SCREENING AND DISCUSSION Arrange a screening for the class to see all or parts of Christopher Quinn's film, "God Grew Tired of Us." After screening the film, have a class discussion using the following questions as a guide:

- Which parts of the film affected you most? Why?
- How did your readings prepare you for the movie?
- How is seeing a movie about the Lost Boys different from reading about them?

If you are using Level 1 in the same classroom, ask students to compare the Lost Boys in the movie with the experiences of children in "Kids on the Run."

INVESTIGATION Have small groups find out more about one of the Lost Boys they have been introduced to. Have students compile information about what has happened to them since the selections were published.

</td></tr>
</table>

The Lost Boys of Sudan

Synthesize, page 125
Students should underline or bracket main ideas in each section. For example, they should underline the sentence in lines 8–9, "These Sudanese boys . . . people of Sudan" for the first section. Passages that remind them of "The Lost Boys" should get a check mark, such as lines 2–7 or line 11. Passages with new information should be marked with a star, such as the information about constructing shacks in lines 19–21. *Remediation Tip* If students struggle with categorizing information, have them work with a partner and review "The Lost Boys" together as they read this article.

✓TestSmart page 126
Answer: B, "Ethiopian soldiers forced them. . . ." If students mark a different choice, have them pinpoint where the information about crossing the Gilo River appears. Point out that the answer is directly in the text, and remind them that they should check their answer choice against the text.

Synthesize, page 126
New Information: Students may note the geographical relationships between African countries, and the exact location of Sudan within Africa.

   Related Information: Students may suggest that the map helps them see the huge distances the Lost Boys traveled, and the paths they trekked on their journeys. *Remediation Tip* Have students return to lines 34–36 and 89–99 in "The Lost Boys," and point out how the information in these sections are reinforced by the map.

Specialized Vocabulary, page 127
Students should underline the following:
- life in the refugee camp was also harsh (line 52)
- malaria (line 53)
- slept on plastic sheets on top of the dirt (line 54)

Clarify & Synthesize, page 127
Students should underline "In their tribal culture . . . village took care of them." (lines 68–69). The Lost Boys would be affected by the plight of the homeless people because they had been homeless themselves before reaching the refugee camp.

Kids on the Run

Synthesize, page 128
Students should check *information about child refugees* and *information about child soldiers.*

✓TestSmart page 129
Answer: C, "Some children are killed in attacks; others become soldiers." Students should circle "two alarming trends that put children on the front lines" (lines 10–11); "First" (line 11); "Second" (line 15).

Synthesize, page 129
Students may say that "Kids on the Run" discusses the impact of war on children all over the world. The article helps readers understand more fully the dangers the Lost Boys encountered. Accept any well-supported answer.

ASSESSMENT PRACTICE II: *p. 130*	
1. C	5. B
2. A	6. A
3. C	7. C
4. B	8. B

In a Strange Land, Trailed by Cameras

Synthesize, page 125
Students should underline or bracket main ideas in each section. For example, they should underline the sentence in line 1, "Christopher Quinn and John Bul Dau are unlikely friends" for the first paragraph. Passages that remind them of "The Lost Boys" should get a check mark, such as lines 4–8.

Synthesize, page 126
Students may underline lines 39–42, which provide details about the refugee camp. Responses should indicate that while life in the camp was often very difficult, with food limited and rationed, it was also where the boys were given the opportunity to come to America.

Specialized Vocabulary, page 126
Students may underline "people will support you" (line 61), "other people" (line 64), "cannot do anything without doing a network" (lines 64–65)

Compare & Make Judgments, page 127
Students may underline the following:
- incredible connection (line 80)
- they had very little resources (line 81)
- very similar to (line 82)
- see first hand, kind of (line 83)

Regardless of their view, students should support their judgments with thoughtful reasons and details from the text.

TestSmart page 127
Answer: D, "He is still troubled. . . ." Have students point out verbs like *running* and *chasing* that show his mind is not at rest.

I Have Had to Learn to Live with Peace

TestSmart page 128
Answer: D, "express feelings"

Synthesize, page 129
Accept well-reasoned responses. Students may suggest that children are deeply affected by war; that these traumatic early experiences may continue to haunt them as they grow up; and that while individual experiences during wartime may vary, they have a great impact on a child's ability to trust and feel connected to others.

Specialized Vocabulary, page 129
Students should circle *vengeance* in line 46 and *revenge* in line 65. *Vengeance* means punishing another as a result of a wrong; *revenge* means much the same: a desire to inflict punishment on another in return for a wrong.

ASSESSMENT PRACTICE II: *p. 130*	
1. C	5. A
2. D	6. B
3. A	7. A
4. D	8. A

LEVEL 1

Guide students through the steps described below under Guided Instruction. You may also wish to go over the rubric on the next page. (Consider modifying the rubric for these students, focusing only on Ideas, Organization, and Conventions.) Give students the entire 45 minutes to draft and review their responses. Point out, however, that in an actual timed writing situation, all steps of the writing process must be completed within the given time frame.

LEVEL 2

Share with students the rubric on the next page. Direct them to complete the entire writing process independently, within the actual 45-minute time frame they have been given.

GUIDED INSTRUCTION

ANALYZE THE PROMPT If necessary, lead the students through the two-step analysis process on page 131. Explain that low scores are often the result of the writer missing a critical piece of the directions. The marked prompt should look like this:

> The Lost Boys faced many struggles in America. <u>Which of them do you think was most preventable?</u> Consider the boys' adjustment to American culture, financial hardship, and loneliness. Then write a problem-solution essay of three to five paragraphs in which you state the problem and discuss how it could be addressed so future refugees will have an easier time. Provide support from at least two of the articles you've read.

- You may want to point out the problems that are listed in the prompt—adjustment to American culture, financial hardship, and loneliness—and explain to students that they should focus their essay on the problem they think is the most preventable.

- *Academic Vocabulary*: Students are asked to write a **problem-solution essay**. Explain that this means that they will need to define or describe a problem, and present solutions that they think will help address the problem.

PLAN YOUR RESPONSE

- Review with students the steps of a timed writing assignment. For a prompt like this, which requires them to provide support, remind them to budget enough time to find examples from the texts. (For a 45-minute assignment, they should probably spend no more than 10 minutes identifying examples.)

- Explain to students that they should first determine which problem they think is most preventable. Have them ask themselves: *Which problem do I know enough about to suggest realistic solutions?*

- Students should list the problem in the outline. They should then find support from the texts they have read and jot down notes or the page numbers in the outline.

- Have students think of and list one or more solutions to the problem in the outline.

WRITE AND REVIEW Review the strategies and suggestions for writing an effective essay. When they have completed their draft, allow peers to comment on how well the students have met the requirements of the prompt.

KEY TRAITS	3 (STRONG)	2 (AVERAGE)	1 (WEAK)
IDEAS	• The thesis statement is focused and presents the problem and the proposed solution. • Relevant details and examples support the solution. • The causes and effects of the problem are explained.	• The thesis statement presents the problem, but it is too broad or too narrow. • Most key ideas are supported by details and examples. • The writer usually explains the causes and effects of the problem.	• The thesis statement is unclear or missing. • Details and examples are not relevant or are too scarce to support the key ideas. • The writer does not explain the causes and effects of the problem.
ORGANIZATION	• The introduction clearly presents the significance of the problem and draws the reader in. • The conclusion summarizes the ideas and draws a conclusion or makes a call to action. • Transitional words and phrases clearly show how ideas connect. • The organization is logical and follows a consistent pattern.	• The introduction presents the significance of the problem, but it does not draw the reader in. • The conclusion summarizes the ideas, but the call to action needs more force. • Most of the transitions work, but a few more are needed. • The organization is logical but occasionally does not follow the established pattern.	• The introduction does not clearly set up what the essay is about. • The essay lacks an identifiable conclusion. • The writer uses few, if any, transitional words. • The organization feels random or disjointed; the reader often feels lost or confused.
VOICE	• The tone and voice are appropriate for the purpose and audience. • The writing reflects active engagement with the problem and its solution.	• The tone and voice are acceptable for the purpose and audience but not strongly individual or direct. • The writing lacks consistent engagement with the topic.	• The voice lacks individuality and is not concerned with or not matched to the audience. • The writing is lifeless or mechanical.
WORD CHOICE	• Words are specific, accurate, and precisely convey the problem and solution.	• Words are adequate and mostly correct.	• Limited vocabulary and/or frequent misuse of parts of speech impair understanding.
SENTENCE FLUENCY	• Sentences vary in length and structure. • Sentence beginnings are varied.	• Sentences do not significantly vary in structure. • Sentence beginnings are sometimes different.	• Sentence structure makes the writing difficult to follow. • Most sentences begin the same way.
CONVENTIONS	• Spelling, capitalization, and punctuation are generally correct. • Grammar and usage are correct. • Paragraphing tends to be correct and reinforces the organization.	• Spelling, capitalization, and punctuation are sometimes uneven. • Grammar and usage are not always correct. • Paragraphing is attempted but is not always sound.	• Spelling, capitalization, and punctuation are frequently incorrect. • Grammar and usage mistakes are frequent and distort meaning. • Paragraphing is missing, irregular, or too frequent.

*Use the Problem-Solution Essay Rubric on the WriteSmart CD if you wish to further modify this chart.

The House on Mango Street

by Sandra Cisneros

SUMMARY:

In the first of three excerpts from *The House on Mango Street,* the narrator recalls how the house her family finally moved into did not live up to her expectations. In the second vignette, she reflects on the life of her great-grandmother, for whom she was named. In the final vignette, the narrator describes how and why she likes to make up stories.

RELATED NONFICTION:

LEVEL 1

BOOK EXCERPT: from *A Home in the Heart: The Story of Sandra Cisneros*

This excerpt from a biography about Sandra Cisneros describes how the author came to discover that the circumstances of the childhood she sought to escape could be a rich source for her writing as an adult. (*Readability*: Average)

LEVEL 2

MAGAZINE ARTICLE: "The Purple Passion of Sandra Cisneros"

To paint her house in historic San Antonio in a palette that reflected Tejano heritage, Sandra Cisneros faced down a local commission. This article recounts her battle over culture and colors. (*Readability*: Average)

FOCUS AND MOTIVATE *p. 133*

FOR ALL STUDENTS

EXPLORE THE BIG QUESTION: *"What STORIES will you tell your children?"*
Invite students to think about how and why stories get passed along from one generation to the next. Discuss how their family stories can shape their lives. Then have students briefly describe stories from their own lives to complete the **List It** activity. Be aware that while some students may welcome the opportunity to share stories from their lives, others may feel less comfortable sharing their personal history.

INTRODUCE THE LESSON Tell students that in these selections, they will gain insight into how Sandra Cisneros's childhood shaped her goals and experiences as an adult, and how she used her experiences in her writing. Then call their attention to the Assessment Goals at the bottom of the page.

ASSESSMENT GOALS

LEVEL 1

- examine an author's perspective in a work of fiction
- use active reading strategies to comprehend text
- study the author's craft in a nonfiction text
- analyze a writing prompt and plan a character description

LEVEL 2

- analyze an author's perspective in a work of fiction
- apply critical thinking skills to analyze text
- analyze the author's craft in a nonfiction text
- dissect a writing prompt and plan a character description

LEVEL 1

Tell students that you will read aloud two passages about a similar topic that reveal differences in each **author's perspective**. Before you read the first passage, tell students to listen closely to identify the **focus**, **tone**, and **word choice** that tell about the author's perspective. Then read the second passage and discuss the same elements of the author's perspective.

Passage 1: Every Friday, I collect my loose change and buy a couple of lottery tickets. Not the instant winner kind, but the big bucks sweepstakes ones. Hey, why take a chance on winning a small pot when you can shoot for the stars? I carefully stash the little slips in my wallet for safekeeping, and then I take few minutes and imagine how I'll feel when I read off the numbers on Saturday and find out . . . I've won! Of course, I haven't ever hit, but the dreaming is a lot of fun.

Passage 2: I can't believe my brother wastes his hard-earned money on lottery tickets every Friday. To my thinking, he might as well just throw his five bucks out the window. Where does his money go? To the state! It's the same as paying extra taxes!

LEVEL 2

If helpful, review how focus, tone, and word choice develop an author's perspective. You may wish to include these additional points:

- An author may choose words that have specific connotations. For example, describing a toddler as "stubborn" sounds negative, but describing the same toddler as "goal-oriented" sounds positive, even humorous.

- An author's perspective may change in a text. An author may want to reveal different perspectives to develop or point out the complexity of a topic, person, or situation.

ADDITIONAL TERMS FOR CRITICAL ANALYSIS

Include the following points in your discussion about **vignette** and **diction:**

- A series of vignettes may be used to build or reinforce larger themes or ideas.

- Diction is often aligned with an author's purpose. A text written to inform will most often use more formal diction than a text written to entertain.

ADDITIONAL RESOURCES
from **McDougal Littell Literature**

STUDENT'S EDITION
Literary Workshop, "Author's Purpose," p. 508
Additional selection questions, p. 575

STANDARDS LESSON FILE: LITERATURE
Lesson 47: Author's Perspective, p. 437
Lesson 42: Word Choice and Diction, p. 399
Lesson 45: Tone, p. 427

RESOURCE MANAGER
Selection Summary, p. 157
Additional Selection Questions, p. 153
Ideas for Extension, p. 154
Reading Check, p. 163
Question Support, p. 164
Selection Test A, p. 167
Selection Test B/C, p. 169

BEST PRACTICES TOOLKIT
Analysis Frame: Literary Nonfiction, p. D48

The House on Mango Street

CLOSE READ

If you are using this selection primarily for **test preparation,** direct students to preview the multiple choice questions on page 139 and the writing prompt on page 140 to help focus their reading. Explain that this technique may be used any time they take a reading test.

✓ TestSmart page 136

Answer: A, "kind, but unrealistic"; If students mark a different choice, review the Tip and ask them to cite evidence in the text that supports their response.

Pause & Reflect, page 136

1. MONITOR Students may circle the following clues on page 135:
• "Each time it seemed there'd be one more of us" (lines 5–6)
• "The water pipes broke . . . the house was too old" (lines 12–13)
Students may respond that the family moved so often because they needed more room for their growing family and because the flats they lived in were in poor shape.
2. DRAW CONCLUSIONS Students should underline "The way she said it made me feel like nothing" in line 47. Responses should suggest that the narrator is embarrassed by the conditions in which she lives, and that having a "real" house would give her a home she could be proud of.

✓ TestSmart Vocabulary, page 137

Answer: A, "plodded"; If needed, have students identify context clues such as "for each step," "her sad brown shoes," and "the house she never liked" in lines 83–85.

Pause & Reflect, page 138

DRAW CONCLUSIONS Students may suggest that writing can be powerful because it allows the author to rise above or move past difficult or painful experiences, even if just for a time. Students may underline lines 92–94.

Big Question page 138

Students may mark either choice but should cite evidence that supports it. Some may point out that she discusses her house most often, and that it is even referenced in the title. Those who feel that her name has a greater effect on her may cite her comment that she wishes for "a name more like the real me, the one nobody sees." Some may even feel that her name and her house are equally important factors that make the narrator feel temporary and like she doesn't belong.

ASSESSMENT PRACTICE I: *p. 139*	
1. A	5. D
2. B	6. C
3. B	7. C
4. A	8. D

Point out to students that the test-taking strategies they learned as they read can be used with the following items:
• Items 2, 4, 5: author's perspective (page 136)
• Item 7: try each possible answer (page 137)

The House on Mango Street

SECOND READ: CRITICAL ANALYSIS

If you are using this selection primarily for **test preparation,** direct students to preview the multiple choice questions on page 139 and the writing prompt on page 140 to help focus their reading. Explain that this technique may be used any time they take a reading test.

Make Inferences, page 135

"They are poor" is the most likely response, but some may respond that since the family was able to buy the house on Mango Street, they could be seen as middle class. Accept reasoned responses, but point out the evidence in lines 12–17 that indicates a level of poverty—they had lived in a house that was too old to fix, making it inadequate for basic needs.

✓ TestSmart page 136

Answer: B, "informal"; If needed, have a volunteer read aloud all or parts of lines 18–27 so students can hear the overall effect of the author's word choices and arrangement of words. You may want to elicit or point out that the author's diction sounds very much like everyday speech.

Visualize & Analyze, page 136

Students should underline words and phrases in lines 29–31 that describe how cramped and unpleasant the house seems, and words and phrases in lines 32–35 that suggest that the house is impersonal and lacks warmth. Responses should reflect the idea that the house does not live up to the narrator's expectations, and that she is disappointed in it.

Connect, page 137

For the first question, accept responses backed by support from the text. Students may suggest that the narrator does not feel that her name reflects who she is in any valid way, and they might underline "a new name . . . the one nobody sees" (lines 77–78). Students will likely have a range of responses for the second question. Some may feel that since people do not choose their own names, there is little effect on their lives. Others may feel that a child's name dictates who he or she will become.

✓ TestSmart Vocabulary, page 137

Answer: A, "plodded"; If needed, have students identify context clues such as "for each step," "her sad brown shoes," and "the house she never liked" in lines 83–85.

Compare, page 138

Repeated: Information about where the narrator lived before Mango Street. New: The author's feeling that she doesn't belong to or connect with the sad house on Mango Street. Both passages reflect the author's belief in the importance of a stable home.

Accept any well-supported answer. Responses may include ideas such as the following:

- She wants to explain her need for, and her lack of, belonging.
- She wants to connect with readers who have had similar experiences.
- She wants to show that her experiences have helped her define her own identity as a writer.

ASSESSMENT PRACTICE I: *p. 139*	
1. B	5. A
2. C	6. D
3. B	7. C
4. B	8. D

Point out to students that the test-taking strategies they learned as they read can be used with the following items:
- Item 2: diction (page 136)
- Item 7: try each possible answer (page 137)

SHORT RESPONSE: PARAGRAPH Use this writing activity to determine whether students understand how focus, word choice, and tone help reveal an author's perspective. Take them through the following steps:

- Have students analyze the prompt. They should notice that they will need to include specific examples from the story.

- Have them review lines 58–71 and complete the chart. Point out that students should use their own words to describe the section's focus. Specific examples of word choices that tell about the author's perspective should be noted in the middle column. They may also cite examples to support their ideas about tone.

- Explain that they should include examples of focus, word choice, and tone in their response.

TEST-TAKER'S TOOLKIT

Author's Perspective		
Focus of the Section	**Word Choice**	**Tone**
• Cisneros was named after her grandmother • what Cisneros knows about her grandmother's life • why Cisneros doesn't want to be like her grandmother	Mexicans "don't like their women strong" "a wild horse of a woman" "threw a sack over her head and carried her off" "as if she were a fancy chandelier" "women who sit their sadness on an elbow"	"would've liked to have known her": regretful "the story goes she never forgave him": wishes she knew more "I don't want to inherit her place by the window": defiant

SAMPLE PARAGRAPH

Lines 58–71 of <u>The House on Mango Street</u> reveal the author's perspective on the injustices women experience in traditional Mexican culture. Cisneros describes her grandmother as "a wild horse" carried off by her grandfather "as if she were a fancy chandelier," and says that Mexicans "don't like their women strong." The author's word choice reflects the impact of this treatment, leaving her grandmother defeated, like "women who sit their sadness on an elbow." The narrator's tone seems regretful and sad that she never knew her grandmother or what her life was really like. Yet she is also defiant in declaring, "I don't want to inherit her place by the window." The short passage shows Cisneros's awareness of cultural traditions and her desire to change them.

SETTING A PURPOSE: Complete the prereading activity on page 141 and review the teaching options below. Then share with your students what their goals will be, and use these goals to set a purpose for reading. Once students are clear on that purpose, have them write a purpose statement at the top of page 142.

TEST PREPARATION: Direct students to read the multiple-choice questions on page 146, as well as the writing prompt on page 147, to help them focus their reading.

LEVEL 1

• from *A Home in the Heart: The Story of Sandra Cisneros*

FOCUS SKILL: ANALYZE AUTHOR'S CRAFT

ACTIVITY: WEB IT

Have students work independently to describe their writing habits in the web on page 141. Invite volunteers to share and discuss their completed webs.

OPTIONS FOR TEACHING

SKILL INSTRUCTION Use "Learn the Skill" at the bottom of page 141 and page R2 in the Nonfiction Skills Handbook to review the focus skill of analyzing author's craft.

> **ADDITIONAL RESOURCES:**
> **STANDARDS LESSON FILE: LITERATURE:** Lesson 46: Style and Syntax, page 437; Lesson 47: Author's Perspective, page 447

DISCUSSION Divide the class into small groups. Have groups discuss the texts they have read, using the following questions to guide the discussion:
- How does cultural background influence people?
- How do reading and writing help you learn about yourself?
- What were your favorite books or stories when you were younger?

If you are using Level 2 in the same classroom, you may want to have mixed groups briefly summarize the selection they have read.

CREATE A BIBLIOGRAPHY Have students investigate other authors who have written novels centering on multicultural experiences, such as Julia Alvarez, An Na, Tanuja Desai Hidier, and Benjamin Alire Sáenz. Have students compile a bibliography of these works.

LEVEL 2

• The Purple Passion of Sandra Cisneros

FOCUS SKILL: ANALYZE AUTHOR'S CRAFT

ACTIVITY: DISCUSS

Have students complete the sentences to tell about an unpopular choice they have made or stand they have taken.

OPTIONS FOR TEACHING

SKILL INSTRUCTION Use "Learn the Skill" at the bottom of page 141 and page R2 in the Nonfiction Skills Handbook to review the focus skill of analyzing author's craft.

> **ADDITIONAL RESOURCES:**
> **STANDARDS LESSON FILE: LITERATURE:** Lesson 46: Style and Syntax, page 437; Lesson 47: Author's Perspective, page 447

JIGSAW LEARNING Divide the class into small groups, each responsible for learning more about Sandra Cisneros's life and work. Then have them share information about the following topics:
- her family, childhood, and places she lived
- her educational and work experience
- her career as a writer
- her current life and experiences

If you are using Level 1 in the same classroom, add *A Home in the Heart: The Story of Sandra Cisneros* to the list of resources for the first three topics.

DEBATE Have small teams debate the controversy outlined in "The Purple Passion of Sandra Cisneros." Encourage students to find additional information about the controversy to bring to the debate.

from *A Home in the Heart: The Story of Sandra Cisneros*

Monitor, page 142
Students should underline the sentence that explains that Cisneros did not fit in at graduate school in lines 3–4. They should underline the sentence that tells how "she began to write about 'third-floor flats, and fear of rats'" in lines 14–15. *Remediation Tip* If students underline the first sentence of each paragraph, guide them to understand that these sentences are topic sentences but do not explain what the problem was or what Cisneros did in response.

Author's Craft, page 142
Responses should center on the author's pattern of organization. By mentioning the "epiphany" first, the author can then go on to provide support to explain how Cisneros came to this realization. It also lets the reader know that Cisneros did find a way to address her difficulties.

Specialized Vocabulary, page 143
Students should circle *communed* in line 34. Possible response: It means "shared knowledge with." The dictionary definition is "to experience a deep emotional or spiritual relationship with something."

Author's Craft, page 143
Students should underline the details that describe how crowded the flats were and the lack of privacy, found in lines 44–47.

Author's Craft, page 144
Students should check "appreciated knowing both Spanish and English." *Remediation Tip* If students check a different response, have them review the beginning of the paragraph on page 143. Guide them to identify the sentence that states that Cisneros felt fortunate to be part of a bilingual family (lines 54–55).

✓TestSmart page 145
Answer: B, "gave her a permanent place to call home"; Students should underline lines 91–93 which describe how the house in Humboldt Park was a "permanent place" in Cisneros's life.

ASSESSMENT PRACTICE II: *p. 146*	
1. B	5. C
2. D	6. A
3. A	7. C
4. D	8. D

The Purple Passion of Sandra Cisneros

Author's Craft, page 142
Students might underline the following:
• consternation (line 14)
• controversial (line 22)
• cultural declaration (line 29)
• political provocation (lines 29–30)
They may circle the following:
• black and white . . . brown and white (lines 9–10)
• a vivid, intense, in-your-face shade of purple (lines 14–16)
Students should mark "playful."

Specialized Vocabulary, page 143
Possible response: They are entrusted with protecting the authenticity of the historic district. *Remediation Tip* If students are unsure, have them reread lines 47–50, which tells about the commission's main responsibility.

Author's Craft, page 143
Opinions will vary. Some may say that the author wants readers to sympathize with Cisneros, since she cites "adoring fans" and compares her to Joan of Arc. Students should support their judgments with evidence from the text. As needed, explain that a journalist is supposed to be fair and to objectively present all sides of a situation.

✓TestSmart page 144
Answer: C, ". . . a home that is uniquely hers." *Remediation Tip* If students mark *A*, about Cisneros's "combative nature," explain that while the quotation does show her strong feelings, it goes on to tell more about her desire for a house that is unique to her, including a place for her "pretty purple petunias."

Draw Conclusions, page 145
Possible response: Cisneros is strong-willed and not afraid of confrontation. It is not enough for her to win a personal battle, if her victory does not help other Tejano people. She demands social justice.

Evaluate, page 145
Accept well-reasoned responses. Students may indicate that they believe that Cisneros is right to use her prestige to bring about cultural change in the community; others may feel that she tried to inject political correctness into a district that is supposed to be defined by its historical past. Those who agree with Cisneros may point out lines 180–185 in which the author explains why the commission's rules may not reflect an understanding of Tejano history. Those who agree with the commission may point out that its rules allow for the uniqueness but require documentation. Responses should give a clear explanation of how they were or were not swayed by the author.

ASSESSMENT PRACTICE II: *p. 146*	
1. D	5. A
2. B	6. B
3. B	7. C
4. A	8. D

LEVEL 1

Guide students through the steps described below under Guided Instruction. You may also wish to go over the rubric on the next page. (Consider modifying the rubric for these students, focusing only on Ideas, Organization, and Conventions.) Give students the entire 30 minutes to draft and review their responses. Point out, however, that in an actual timed writing situation, all steps of the writing process must be completed within the given time frame.

LEVEL 2

Share with students the rubric on the next page. Direct them to complete the entire writing process independently, within the actual 30-minute time frame they have been given.

GUIDED INSTRUCTION

ANALYZE THE PROMPT If necessary, lead the students through the two-step analysis process on page 147. Explain that low scores are often the result of the writer missing a critical piece of the directions. The marked prompt should look like this:

> Sandra Cisneros overcame the difficulties of her childhood and used her experiences to become a successful writer. Think of someone you have read about or know personally who has used a specific skill or talent to overcome great hardship. Write an essay in which you describe the person's background, personality, and accomplishments. Make your description so vivid that your readers will feel like they know this person.

- *Academic Vocabulary*: Point out that in a **description**, students should include facts and details that present a clear picture to the reader.
- Explain to students that they will need to describe both the person's hardship and how he or she used specific talents or skills to overcome that difficulty.

PLAN YOUR RESPONSE

- Review with students the steps of a timed writing assignment. For a prompt like this, which requires students to describe someone, remind them to budget enough time to gather specific details. (For a 30-minute assignment, they should probably spend no more than 5 minutes identifying details about their subject.)
- Have students complete a planning chart like the one on page 147. Tell them to use the information in the completed chart to structure their description.

WRITE AND REVIEW Review the idea of focusing on their subject's special qualities. When they have completed their draft, allow peers to comment on how well the students have met the requirements of the prompt.

RUBRIC FOR TIMED WRITING*

KEY TRAITS	3 (STRONG)	2 (AVERAGE)	1 (WEAK)
IDEAS	• The thesis statement is focused and clearly presents the subject of the description. • Details and examples support each key idea. • The writer clearly explains the relevance of the examples.	• The thesis statement is too broad or too narrow but loosely presents the subject of the description. • Most key ideas are supported by details and examples. • The writer explains how most examples are relevant to the thesis.	• The thesis statement is unclear or missing. • Details and examples are not relevant or are too scarce to support the key ideas. • The ideas are repetitive or lack a clear point.
ORGANIZATION	• The introduction clearly presents the focus of the description and engages the reader. • The conclusion summarizes the description and draws a conclusion or offers an observation. • Transitional words and phrases are suitable for the description. • The organization is logical and follows a consistent pattern.	• The introduction presents an identifiable focus of the description but does not engage the reader. • The conclusion summarizes the description but only restates what has been said. • Most of the transitions work, but a few more are needed. • The organization is logical but may have occasional inconsistencies.	• The introduction does not clearly set up what the essay is about. • The essay lacks an identifiable conclusion. • The writer uses few, if any, transitional words. • The organization feels random or disjointed; the reader often feels lost or confused.
VOICE	• The tone and voice are appropriate for the purpose and audience. • The writing reflects active engagement with the topic.	• The tone and voice are acceptable. • The writing lacks consistent engagement with the topic.	• The voice is not matched to the audience. • The writing reflects no engagement with the topic.
WORD CHOICE	• Vivid sensory words are used to convey the description.	• Some sensory words are used to convey the description.	• Limited vocabulary and/or frequent misuse of parts of speech impair understanding.
SENTENCE FLUENCY	• Sentences vary in length and structure. • Sentence beginnings are varied.	• Sentences do not significantly vary in structure. • Sentence beginnings are mostly the same.	• Repetitive sentences structure, fragments, and run-on sentences make the writing difficult to follow. • Most or all sentences begin the same way.
CONVENTIONS	• Spelling, capitalization, and punctuation are correct. • Grammar and usage are correct. • Paragraphing tends to be correct and reinforces the organization.	• Spelling, capitalization, and punctuation are sometimes uneven. • Grammar and usage are not always correct. • Paragraphing is attempted but is not always sound.	• Spelling, capitalization, and punctuation are frequently incorrect. • Grammar and usage mistakes distort meaning. • Paragraphing is missing, irregular, or too frequent.

*Use the Description Rubric on the WriteSmart CD if you wish to further modify this chart.

I Have a Dream
by Dr. Martin Luther King Jr.

SUMMARY:

In his historic "I Have a Dream" speech, delivered at the Lincoln Memorial in 1963, Dr. Martin Luther King Jr. presents a promise of freedom that has yet to be realized. He urges listeners to continue to press for freedom in the form of racial equality. He concludes by sharing his vision of an America in which racial differences do not matter and all people are "free at last."

RELATED NONFICTION:

LEVEL 1

TEXTBOOK EXCERPT: "Kennedy, Johnson, and Civil Rights"
This excerpt from a social studies textbook traces how civil rights issues and events prompted Presidents Kennedy and Johnson to advocate for passage of the Civil Rights Act of 1964. (*Readability*: Average)

BOOK EXCERPT: from *A Dream of Freedom*
This book excerpt describes background events that shaped the way Dr. Martin Luther King Jr. delivered his famous speech at the March on Washington on August 28, 1963. (*Readability*: Average)

LEVEL 2

PROGRAM: "March on Washington for Jobs and Freedom"
This primary source, the program from the 1963 March on Washington, details the day's program, speakers, and their aims. (*Readability*: Challenging)

NEWSPAPER ARTICLE: "'I Have a Dream . . .': Peroration by Dr. King Sums up a Day the Capital Will Remember"
This 1963 article from the *New York Times* is a primary source that documents the March on Washington and Dr. Martin Luther King Jr.'s speech. (*Readability*: Average)

FOCUS AND MOTIVATE *p. 149*

FOR ALL STUDENTS

EXPLORE THE BIG QUESTION: *"Can a DREAM change the world?"*
Discuss the question with students, and encourage them to give examples of how individual actions have made a difference in the world. Then have them complete the **Web It** activity, focusing on one vision and concrete ideas that could help bring it about.

INTRODUCE THE LESSON Tell students that in these selections, they will learn more about events of the Civil Rights Era and details about Dr. King's speech and the March on Washington. Then call their attention to the Assessment Goals at the bottom of the page.

ASSESSMENT GOALS

LEVEL 1

- identify elements of an argument and persuasive language in a speech
- use active reading strategies to comprehend text
- compare sources about a topic
- analyze a writing prompt and plan a summary

LEVEL 2

- examine elements of an argument and persuasive language in a speech
- apply critical thinking skills to analyze text
- analyze nonfiction primary sources
- analyze a writing prompt and plan a summary

LEVEL 1

Use the graphic organizer to work with students to develop a **claim** on a topic of interest to them, such as: *Starting the school day two hours later would be better for high school students.* Encourage students to think of at least two reasons that would support this claim, and record them in the organizer. Explain that strong **support** would be needed to make their **argument** convincing. Invite students to suggest evidence that would support the claim.

As students make their suggestions for reasons and evidence, point out examples of **persuasive language**, strong reasoning, and language that has emotional appeal but is weaker in hard evidence.

LEVEL 2

If helpful, review the definitions of argument, claim, support, and persuasive language. You may wish to include these additional points:

FOR ARGUMENT AND CLAIM

- A strong argument is based in reason, not just emotion.
- The claim is often stated at the beginning and again at the end of an argument.

FOR PERSUASIVE LANGUAGE

- Using persuasive language is not necessarily a sign of a weak argument. An argument can be bolstered by persuasive language regardless of its validity.
- Make a note of examples of strong persuasive language, and consider why you find it persuasive.

ADDITIONAL TERMS FOR CRITICAL ANALYSIS

To reinforce understanding of **emotional and ethical appeals**, include the following points in your discussion of the terms:

- Emotional appeals are used frequently in advertising and marketing, but they can also be used effectively in reasoned arguments.
- Ethical appeals are used most frequently to persuade people to change the way they feel or act.

ADDITIONAL RESOURCES
from McDougal Littell Literature

STUDENT'S EDITION
Literary Workshop, "Argument and Persuasion," p. 594
Additional selection questions, p. 608

STANDARDS LESSON FILE: READING AND INFORMATIONAL TEXTS
Lesson 14: Elements of an Argument, p. 299
Lesson 15: Persuasive Techniques, p. 309

RESOURCE MANAGER
Selection Summary, p. 25
Additional Selection Questions, p. 21
Ideas for Extension, p. 22
Vocabulary Study, p. 31
Vocabulary Practice, p. 32
Reading Check, p. 34
Question Support, p. 35
Selection Test A, p. 39
Selection Test B/C, p. 41

BEST PRACTICES TOOLKIT
Persuasive Essay, p. C31
Analysis Frame: Persuasion, p. D44

FOR ALL STUDENTS

VOCABULARY IN CONTEXT Read aloud the context phrases below and show students how to use context clues to figure out meaning. Once students have offered their own suggestions, review the actual definitions.

SELECTION VOCABULARY

momentous *(adj.)*: of great importance (line 4)

default *(v.)*: to fail to keep a promise, especially a promise to repay a loan (line 22)

legitimate *(adj.)*: justifiable; reasonable (line 38)

militancy *(n.)*: the act of aggressively supporting a political or social cause (line 55)

inextricably *(adv.)*: in a way impossible to untangle (line 59)

exalted *(adj.)*: raised up **exalt** *v.* (line 103)

CONTEXT PHRASES

1. a **momentous** occasion

2. miss payments and **default** on a loan

3. a **legitimate** excuse to miss school

4. turned from protest to **militancy**

5. two evils **inextricably** joined

6. felt **exalted** listening to great music

FOR ENGLISH LEARNERS

Make sure students are familiar with the following terms and references that appear in this story.

Idioms Review and discuss the following expressions with students.
- **cooling off** (lines 31–32): calming down
- **blow off steam** (line 42): release anger
- **rude awakening** (line 43): shocking realization
- **business as usual** (line 43): the normal routine
- **tied up with** (line 58): connected to
- **speed up that day** (line 129): make a time come more quickly

Cultural References Review the following terms about United States history with students.

- **the Constitution and the Declaration of Independence** (lines 17–18): historic documents from the late 18th century that provide frameworks for our country's government and politics
- **signs stating For Whites Only** (lines 69–70): posted statements that supported segregation before the passage of the Civil Rights Act of 1964
- **"My country 'tis of thee, . . . let freedom ring."** (lines 115–117): lyrics from a well-known patriotic song
- **the old Negro spiritual** (lines 131–132): a familiar gospel song from African-American religious services

I Have a Dream

CLOSE READ

If you are using this selection primarily for **test preparation,** direct students to preview the multiple choice questions on page 156 and the writing prompt on page 157 to help focus their reading. Explain that this technique may be used any time they take a reading test.

Monitor, page 151

Students should underline the following:
"crippled by the manacles . . . chains of discrimination" (lines 9–10)
"lives on a lonely island . . . material prosperity" (lines 11–12)
"finds himself in exile in his own land" (lines 13–14)

Monitor, page 152

As needed, help students show how King uses metaphors of finance to help people understand his belief that African Americans have not received what is due to them. Students might underline the following:
defaulted (line 22)
promissory note (lines 22–23)
a bad check, . . . marked "insufficient funds" (lines 24–25)
bank of justice is bankrupt (line 26)
cash this check (line 28)
riches . . . security of justice (line 29)

✓TestSmart page 152

Answer: D, "The revolt will go on. . . ." If students choose another answer, point out and explain that the question centers on summarizing what King is saying in lines 41–46.

Pause & Reflect, page 153

1. *ANALYZE* Students should underline details that describe the injustices that African Americans still face. *Remediation Tip* Have students look for details that follow the repeated phrase "we can never be satisfied as long as" in lines 62–73.
2. *DRAW CONCLUSIONS* Students should underline the phrase "Go back to." They should suggest that King is trying to persuade people that they should not give up on the struggle for civil rights once they return to their homes in different parts of the country.

✓TestSmart Vocabulary, page 154

Answer: C, "a fertile spot . . ."

Evaluate, page 154

Students should check *more persuasive.* If students check *less persuasive,* ask them to offer support for that response.

Pause & Reflect, page 155

INTERPRET Students should circle "let freedom ring." They may suggest that the phrase appeals to emotions such as hope, inspiration, and determination.

Big Question page 155

Responses will likely suggest that King outlines his ideas and vision so vividly and powerfully that it caused many to truly understand and work to end the injustices facing African Americans.

ASSESSMENT PRACTICE I: *p. 156*	
1. B	5. C
2. D	6. A
3. C	7. C
4. D	8. D

Point out to students that the test-taking strategies they learned as they read can be used with the following items:
• Items 1, 2, 4: best answer (page 152)
• Items 7, 8: context clues (page 154)

I Have a Dream

SECOND READ: CRITICAL ANALYSIS

If you are using this selection primarily for **test preparation,** direct students to preview the multiple choice questions on page 156 and the writing prompt on page 157 to help focus their reading. Explain that this technique may be used any time they take a reading test.

Compare, page 151

Students may suggest emotions such as shame, sadness, or anger. They should note that these emotions are very different from the emotions of hope and inspiration King appeals to in the closing paragraphs. *Remediation Tip* Have students compare the images they "see" in the boxed text—of imprisonment and loneliness with those in the closing text, ones of freedom and unity.

Make Inferences, page 152

Students should underline lines 19–21, "This note was the promise . . . life, liberty, and the pursuit of happiness." They should check *our belief in justice and certain unalienable rights.* If students check another choice, ask them to offer support from the text.

Analyze, page 152

Students should underline "Now is the time . . . to make justice a reality for all of God's children" (lines 32–37). If students underline a different sentence, have them determine whether it is a claim that King returns to throughout the speech.

Make Judgments, page 153

Students should underline details in lines 62–73 that show the many ways that African Americans face injustice, such as from police brutality, discrimination, and the loss of dignity. Accept all responses about which passage is more persuasive, as long as they are supported by valid reasoning.

✓TestSmart page 153

Answer: C, "Have hope. . . ." If students choose another response, use the Tip and have them summarize the passage by restating it in their own words.

✓TestSmart Vocabulary, page 154

Answer: C, "a fertile spot . . ."

Evaluate, page 155

As King's speech employs effective use of evidence, emotional appeals, and ethical appeals, accept any response that is supported by clear reasoning. Invite students to share their responses and discuss how individuals can have different responses to different types of persuasion.

Big Question page 155

Responses will likely suggest that King outlines his ideas and vision so vividly and powerfully that it caused many to truly understand and work to end the injustices facing African Americans.

ASSESSMENT PRACTICE I: *p. 156*	
1. B	5. C
2. D	6. A
3. C	7. B
4. D	8. D

Point out to students that the test-taking strategies they learned as they read can be used with the following items:
- Item 2: summarize (page 153)
- Items 7, 8: context clues (page 154)

SHORT RESPONSE: SUMMARY Use this writing activity to determine whether students understand the concept of a claim supported by reasons and evidence. Take them through the following steps:

- Have students analyze the prompt. They should notice that they will be focusing on lines 47–61.
- Tell them to reread lines 47–61, and then write a statement in the chart that summarizes King's principal claim.
- Have students fill in the chart with two more reasons that support King's claim. Explain that since his words are so powerful, they should quote his words.
- Explain that they can use their completed chart as a guide to write their summaries.

TEST-TAKER'S TOOLKIT

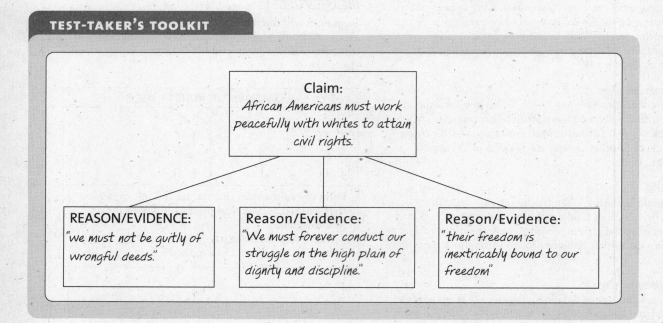

SAMPLE SUMMARY

In lines 47–61 of "I Have a Dream," Dr. Martin Luther King Jr. sets forth his belief that African Americans must work peacefully with whites to push for civil rights. To support his claim, he argues that violence or "wrongful deeds" will not help, and that African Americans "must forever conduct our struggle on the high plain of dignity and discipline." King further supports his claim by explaining that the freedom of white America "is inextricably bound to our freedom" and that only by working together can all Americans be free.

SETTING A PURPOSE Complete the prereading activity on page 158 and review the teaching options below. Then share with your students what their goals will be, and use these goals to set a purpose for reading. Once students are clear on that purpose, have them write a purpose statement at the top of page 159.

TEST PREPARATION Direct students to read the multiple-choice questions on page 164, as well as the writing prompt on page 165, to help them focus their reading.

LEVEL 1

- ## Kennedy, Johnson, and Civil Rights

- ## *from* A Dream of Freedom

FOCUS SKILL: COMPARE SOURCES

ACTIVITY: CHART IT

Have students complete the first two columns of the K-W-L chart the day before you assign the reading. Have them fill out the third column after reading.

OPTIONS FOR TEACHING

SKILL INSTRUCTION Use "Learn the Skill" at the bottom of page 158 and page R2 in the Nonfiction Skills Handbook to review the focus skill of comparing sources.

> **ADDITIONAL RESOURCES:**
> **STANDARDS LESSON FILE:** READING AND INFORMATIONAL TEXTS: Lesson 12: Comparing and Contrasting, page 111

JIGSAW LEARNING Divide the class into small groups, each responsible for learning and then sharing information about one of the following topics:
- Jim Crow laws
- The March on Washington in 1963
- Events that led to the passage of the Civil Rights Act of 1964

If you are using Level 2 in the same classroom, have students find out how the March was covered in the media, and use the newspaper article "Peroration by Dr. King" as a resource.

INVESTIGATION Have students investigate aspects of Dr. Martin Luther King Jr.'s life, such as his writings, his death, and his legacy and contributions.

LEVEL 2

- ## March on Washington for Jobs and Freedom

- ## "I Have a Dream . . .": Peroration by Dr. King Sums Up a Day the Capital Will Remember

FOCUS SKILL: ANALYZE PRIMARY SOURCES

ACTIVITY: LIST IT

Have students complete the activity on page 158 and compile a list of questions a reporter might ask someone who attended the March on Washington.

OPTIONS FOR TEACHING

SKILL INSTRUCTION Use "Learn the Skill" at the bottom of page 158 and page R2 in the Nonfiction Skills Handbook to review the focus skill of analyzing primary sources.

> **ADDITIONAL RESOURCES:**
> **STANDARDS LESSON FILE:** READING AND INFORMATIONAL TEXTS: Lesson 14: Synthesizing Information, page 133

JIGSAW LEARNING Divide the class into small groups, each responsible for learning and then sharing information about one of the following topics:
- How the March was organized
- How the March was covered by the media
- The effects of the March

If you are using Level 1 in the same classroom, have students research events that led to the March, and use "Kennedy, Johnson, and Civil Rights" as a resource.

DISCUSSION Have a class discussion about how life has or has not changed for African Americans since the passage of the Civil Rights Act of 1964.

Kennedy, Johnson, and Civil Rights

Compare Sources, page 159
Students should check *objective facts. Remediation Tip*: If students are unfamiliar with the meaning of *objective,* remind them that they can use the word *facts* as a context clue. Elicit from students that while a history or social sciences textbook may include quotations or other information that reveals personal statements, its primary goal is to provide a full picture of events.

Specialized Vocabulary, page 159
Possible responses:
- *desegregate:* get rid of segregation; bring races together
- *segregationist:* someone who wants to keep races separate
- *integration:* the act of bringing together
Have students consult a dictionary to confirm definitions.

Clarify, page 160
Students should underline the two sentences in lines 45–47 that tell about how the use of firehoses and dogs on marchers horrified television viewers. Student responses should suggest that these shocking events and images allowed many people to see the levels of brutality in the response to protests and prompted them to call for change.

Compare Sources, page 161
Students should check *vivid sensory descriptions, quotations,* and *facts. Remediation Tip*: If students fail to check one of the correct choices, review the text together and point out the missed detail.

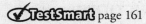 page 161

Answer: A, "President Johnson fulfilled. . . ." Students should underline the first sentence in the first, second, and fourth paragraphs, and the second sentence of the third paragraph.

from a Dream of Freedom

Clarify, page 162
Students should underline the sentence in lines 13–15 that refers to General Sherman. Possible response: they described the possibility of widespread violence and destruction.

Analyze, page 163
Possible response: King was a thoughtful person and a sensitive speaker because he realized that his prepared words did not match the mood of the audience. Students should underline words and phrases that support their ideas.

Compare Sources, page 163
Accept responses that indicate an idea unique to the second source. Possible response: that the speech Dr. King delivered was different from what he had originally prepared to say

ASSESSMENT PRACTICE II: *p. 164*	
1. D	5. C
2. C	6. B
3. A	7. C
4. A	8. B

March on Washington for Jobs and Freedom

Primary Sources, page 159
Students should place a star next to the following names: The Very Rev. Patrick O'Boyle, Dr. Eugene Carson Blake, Rabbi Uri Miller, Rabbi Joachim Prinz, and The Rev. Dr. Martin Luther King, Jr. Students will likely conclude that religion or faith played a major role in the March on Washington.

Analyze, page 160
Students should check *formal, dignified,* and *sincere.* If students check other words, ask them to offer support for their answer.

Primary Sources, page 160
Responses will most likely indicate that the organizers wanted to clarify to participants and observers that their intention was to have a March that was "disciplined and purposeful."

Specialized Vocabulary, page 161
Students should underline the context clues "compromise" in Demand 1 and "when any constitutional right is violated" in Demand 6. Definition for *filibuster*: "the use of obstructionist tactics to delay legislation." Definition for *injunctive suit*: "a lawsuit intended to prohibit a party from a specific course of action."

Make Inferences, page 161
Accept any well-supported response; students will most likely infer that the disclaimer was needed to make it clear that not every organization involved in the March supported every item on the list of demands.

"I Have a Dream . . .": Peroration by Dr. King Sums Up a Day the Capital Will Remember

✓**TestSmart** page 162
Answer: A, "Roger Williams"; *Remediation Tip* While the author compares King to all of the men listed as answer choices, point out that only Roger Williams is a religious reformer. Remind students to read test questions carefully.

Primary Sources, page 163
Students may underline details such as "Negro" (lines 83 or 89) and infer that it was an acceptable term to use in the early 1960s; "covered by television and the press" (line 85) and infer that such coverage reflected a fairly new practice.

Synthesize, page 163
Responses will differ depending on each student's prior knowledge.

ASSESSMENT PRACTICE II: *p. 164*	
1. C	5. D
2. B	6. B
3. A	7. C
4. D	8. A

LEVEL 1

Guide students through the steps described below under Guided Instruction. You may also wish to go over the rubric on the next page. (Consider modifying the rubric for these students, focusing only on Ideas, Organization, and Conventions.) Give students the entire 45 minutes to draft and review their responses. Point out, however, that in an actual timed writing situation, all steps of the writing process must be completed within the given time frame.

LEVEL 2

Share with students the rubric on the next page. Direct them to complete the entire writing process independently, within the actual 45-minute time frame they have been given.

GUIDED INSTRUCTION

ANALYZE THE PROMPT If necessary, lead the students through the two-step analysis process on page 165. Explain that low scores are often the result of the writer missing a critical piece of the directions. The marked prompt should look like this:

In 1963, 250,000 people joined the March on Washington to pursue a shared dream of equality. Write a <u>summary</u> that (describes the goals of the March) and (tells what it was like). In your essay, be sure to (include details from) Dr. Martin Luther King Jr.'s speech, ("I Have a Dream," and from the related readings).

- *Academic Vocabulary*: Students are asked to write a **summary.** Remind students that a summary should only include key main ideas and important details.

- Point out to students that if they choose, they can make a list to help them restate the prompt. Responses should include the type of writing, what it should cover, and what specific information it should include.

PLAN YOUR RESPONSE

- Review with students the steps of a timed writing assignment. For a prompt like this, which requires them to include details from the readings, remind them to budget enough time to find details. (They should probably spend no more than 10 minutes identifying details.)

- Review the steps under *Organize your information* to help students see that this section provides a clear set of instructions to help them prepare their essay.

WRITE AND REVIEW Point out to students that when they refer to each reading, they should use clear descriptions so that the reader knows which reading is being cited. If time allows, discuss ideas for these descriptions, but note that the related readings vary between levels. When they have completed their draft, allow peers to comment on how well the students have met the requirements of the prompt.

RUBRIC FOR TIMED WRITING*

KEY TRAITS	3 (STRONG)	2 (AVERAGE)	1 (WEAK)
IDEAS	• The thesis statement clearly identifies the main points of the summary. • Relevant details and examples support each key idea.	• The thesis statement presents the subject of the summary, but it is too broad or too narrow. • Most key ideas are supported by details and examples.	• The thesis statement is unclear or missing. • Details and examples are not relevant or too scarce to support the key ideas.
ORGANIZATION	• The introduction clearly presents the topic of the summary. • The conclusion clearly shows the significance of the summary. • Transitional words and phrases clearly show how ideas connect. • The organization is logical and follows a consistent pattern.	• The introduction presents the subject of the summary but does not draw the reader in. • The conclusion does not make the significance of the summary entirely clear. • Most of the transitions work, but a few more are needed. • The organization shows some logic but does not follow a consistent pattern.	• The introduction does not clearly set up what the essay is about. • The essay lacks an identifiable conclusion. • The writer uses few, if any, transitional words. • The organization feels random or disjointed; the reader often feels lost or confused.
VOICE	• The tone and voice are appropriate for the purpose and audience. • The writing reflects active engagement with the subject of the summary.	• The tone and voice are acceptable for the purpose and audience but not strongly individual or direct. • The writing lacks consistent engagement with the subject of the summary.	• The voice lacks individuality and is not concerned with or not matched to the audience. • The writing is lifeless or mechanical.
WORD CHOICE	• Words are specific, accurate, and convey precise meaning.	• Words are adequate and mostly correct.	• Limited vocabulary and/or frequent misuse of parts of speech impair understanding.
SENTENCE FLUENCY	• Sentences vary in length and structure. • Sentence beginnings are varied.	• Sentences do not significantly vary in structure. • Sentence beginnings are mostly the same.	• Repetitive sentence structure, fragments, and run-on sentences make the writing difficult to follow. • Most or all sentences begin the same way.
CONVENTIONS	• Spelling, capitalization, and punctuation are correct. • Grammar and usage are correct. • Paragraphing tends to be correct and reinforces the organization.	• Spelling, capitalization, and punctuation are sometimes uneven. • Grammar and usage are not always correct. • Paragraphing is attempted but is not always sound.	• Spelling, capitalization, and punctuation are frequently incorrect. • Grammar and usage mistakes distort meaning. • Paragraphing is missing, irregular, or too frequent.

*Use the Subject Analysis Rubric on the WriteSmart CD if you wish to further modify this chart.

My Papa's Waltz
by Theodore Roethke

Grape Sherbet
by Rita Dove

I Ask My Mother to Sing
by Li-Young Lee

SUMMARIES:

"My Papa's Waltz" In this poem, the speaker shares a memory about his energetic romps with his father before bedtime.

"I Ask My Mother to Sing" The speaker of this poem describes how his mother and grandmother tearfully sing about a beautiful place in China that he has never seen.

"Grape Sherbet" In this poem, the speaker recalls a Memorial Day cookout when her father made grape sherbet. She reflects upon the importance of cherishing family memories and honoring the dead.

RELATED NONFICTION:

LEVEL 1

ONLINE ARTICLE: "Memory"
This article discusses memory and how our brains process and store information so that it can be retrieved later. (*Readability*: Average)

ONLINE ARTICLE: "The Family Memories Project"
Methods used to preserve and pass on personal and family information and memories are outlined in this online article. (*Readability*: Easy)

LEVEL 2

ONLINE ARTICLE: "Messing with Your Mind"
According to this article, research shows that our memories are not a collection of objective facts, but that they can be shaped by ourselves and others. (*Readability*: Average)

ONLINE ARTICLE: "Linking Smell and Memory"
This article presents intriguing research that explores how and why smells from our childhood tend to evoke nostalgic emotions. (*Readability*: Challenging)

FOCUS AND MOTIVATE *p. 167*

FOR ALL STUDENTS

EXPLORE THE BIG QUESTION: *"Who lives in your MEMORY?"*
Discuss the question with students, prompting them to recall a specific event or moment they shared with others. Then have them complete the **Web It** activity, listing sensory details from their memories.

INTRODUCE THE LESSON Tell students that through these selections, they will learn more about the importance of memory and how it works. Then call their attention to the Assessment Goals at the bottom of the page.

ASSESSMENT GOALS

LEVEL 1

- identify poetic elements, such as imagery and figurative language
- use active reading strategies to comprehend text
- identify patterns of organization in nonfiction
- examine a writing prompt and plan an essay to analyze poetry

LEVEL 2

- analyze poetic elements, such as imagery and figurative language
- apply critical thinking skills to analyze text
- analyze patterns of organization in nonfiction text
- examine a writing prompt and plan an essay to analyze poetry

LEVEL 1

To help students identify various types of **figurative language,** present a number of examples like those in the sentences that follow. Have students identify **simile, metaphor, personification,** and **hyperbole.** Then ask students to describe how the figurative language makes the ideas come to life.

> The old school bus coughed and snorted in the cold, brittle air. (personification)
>
> The path to my sister's closet was a confusing maze of books, magazines, and dirty clothes. (metaphor)
>
> It will take me years to get all of this homework done! (hyperbole)
>
> Kelly's laughter floated like soap bubbles above the crowd. (simile)
>
> Ms. Sheenan's reminder set off a ringing alarm in my head. (metaphor)
>
> Marco's plans for the day were about as organized as a pile of leaves on a windy day. (simile)

LEVEL 2

If helpful, review the definitions of **imagery,** simile, metaphor, personification, and hyperbole. You may wish to include these additional points:

FOR IMAGERY

- Because imagery appeals to the senses, its use in poetry grabs the reader's attention and goes beyond the literal meanings of the words, often creating an emotional connection between words and ideas.

- By establishing a vivid image and developing it throughout a poem, a poet is often able to create layers of meaning.

FOR FIGURATIVE LANGUAGE

- Like imagery, figurative language is used to deepen meaning beyond the literal meaning of the words a poet chooses.

- Poets use figurative language that aids readers in making fresh, unique connections.

ADDITIONAL TERMS FOR CRITICAL ANALYSIS

To reinforce students' understanding of **lyric poetry,** include the following points in your discussion:

- All three of the poems employ a single speaker, each recollecting memories of a time or an event.

- Two of the poems—"My Papa's Waltz" and "I Ask My Mother to Sing"—reference music in their titles. All three poems have a strong melodic rhythm that adds to the musical qualities of lyric poetry.

ADDITIONAL RESOURCES
from **McDougal Littell Literature**

STUDENT'S EDITION
Literary Workshop, "The Language of Poetry," p. 668

Additional selection questions, p. 682

STANDARDS LESSON FILE: LITERATURE
Lesson 18: Narrative vs. Lyric Poetry, p. 165

Lesson 28: Imagery, p. 265

Lesson 29: Simile and Metaphor, p. 275

Lesson 30: Personification, p. 285

RESOURCE MANAGER
Additional Selection Questions, p. 21

Ideas for Extension, p. 22

Question Support, p. 29

Selection Test A, p. 33

Selection Test B/C, p. 35

BEST PRACTICES TOOLKIT
Evaluating a Poem, p. D17

Core Analysis Frame: Poetry, p. D34

My Papa's Waltz

CLOSE READ

If you are using this selection primarily for **test preparation**, direct students to preview the multiple choice questions on page 172 and the writing prompt on page 173 to help focus their reading. Explain that this technique may be used any time they take a reading test.

Pause & Reflect, page 169
1. *MAKE INFERENCES* She doesn't approve of it. Students should underline lines 7–8, "My mother's countenance/ Could not unfrown itself." She may think that it is dangerous or too rowdy.
2. *MAKE INFERENCES* Students might circle any of the following: "The hand that held my wrist" (line 9), "My right ear scraped a buckle" (line 12), "You beat time on my head" (line 13), or "Still clinging to your shirt" (line 16). Students may suggest that the boy and his father have a rough physical relationship, but it is also one of affection. *Remediation Tip* If students have difficulty recognizing the complexity of the relationship, point out clues such those in lines 3–4 and 15–16.

I Ask My Mother to Sing

TestSmart page 170

Answer: A, simile *Remediation Tip* If students choose an incorrect answer, review the academic vocabulary. Prompt them to note that the word *like* in line 4 signals a simile.

Pause & Reflect, page 170
VISUALIZE Students may circle lines 7–8 describing rain on a picnic and lines 10–12 about waterlilies filling with rain.

Grape Sherbet

Clarify, page 171
His "masterpiece" is homemade grape sherbet. Students should check the second choice, metaphor. *Remediation Tip* Review the meaning of the academic vocabulary to be certain that students understand each term.

Pause & Reflect, page 171
Students may underline "like salt on a melon" in line 15 and "It's just how we imagined lavender/ would taste" in lines 17–18.

Big Question page 171
Responses will likely suggest the speaker's father and mother in "My Papa's Waltz," the speaker's mother and grandmother in "I Ask My Mother to Sing," and the speaker's father in "Grape Sherbet."

ASSESSMENT PRACTICE I: *p. 172*	
1. C	5. A
2. A	6. D
3. B	7. B
4. C	8. D

Point out to students that the test-taking strategies they learned as they read can be used with the following item:
• Item 7: identify figurative language (page 170)

My Papa's Waltz

SECOND READ: CRITICAL ANALYSIS

If you are using this selection primarily for **test preparation**, direct students to preview the multiple choice questions on page 172 and the writing prompt on page 173 to help focus their reading. Explain that this technique may be used any time they take a reading test.

Interpret, page 169
Students may circle the following: "whiskey on your breath" (line 1), "death" (line 3), "battered" (line 10), "beat" (line 13). They may suggest that the memory is complex but not necessarily unhappy. Accept all supported responses.

Evaluate, page 169
Students will most likely rate the first and third categories at or near 5; the second category will most likely be rated lower, as personal thoughts are not directly expressed in the poem. *Remediation Tip* If students mark very different responses, ask them to cite evidence in the text to support their responses.

I Ask My Mother to Sing

TestSmart page 170

Answer: A, simile. If students choose another response, use the Tip and have them review the academic vocabulary.

Grape Sherbet

Analyze, page 171
Students may circle "swirled snow, gelled light" (line 3), "like salt on a melon" (line 15), and "how we imagined lavender / would taste" (lines 17–18), and should indicate that the imagery appeals to sight and taste.

Interpret, page 171
The speaker feels appreciation and gratitude. *Remediation Tip* If students have difficulty, point out the repeated references to remembering those who have died (lines 1, 10, 22–23), and the last three lines of the poem.

Big Question page 171
In "My Papa's Waltz," the speaker is remembering a personal family event, one that perhaps occurred repeatedly; in "I Ask My Mother to Sing," the speaker is making a connection to his family's Chinese heritage; in "Grape Sherbet," the speaker is expressing her realization that the Memorial Day celebration had far greater meaning than she was aware of at the time.

ASSESSMENT PRACTICE I: *p. 172*	
1. C	5. D
2. A	6. B
3. A	7. B
4. C	8. D

Point out to students that the test-taking strategies they learned as they read can be used with the following items:
• Items 3, 6, 7: academic vocabulary (page 170)

SHORT RESPONSE: PARAGRAPH Use this writing activity to determine whether students understand imagery and how it is used in poetry. Take them through the following steps:

- Have students analyze the prompt. They should notice that they are being asked to write a paragraph about an image in one of the poems they have read.

- Have them complete the graphic organizer, noting images used in each poem. Encourage students to quote words and phrases from each poem. After they have completed the organizer, they will choose one image to write about.

- Remind students that the prompt asks them to tell which sense or senses the image appeals to, and how this image helps bring the scene to life.

- Explain that in order to help the reader, students should include in their paragraphs exact words and phrases from the poem that describe the image.

TEST-TAKER'S TOOLKIT

IMAGERY		
"My Papa's Waltz"	**"I Ask My Mother to Sing"**	**"Grape Sherbet"**
• elements of waltzing: "the pans slid from the kitchen shelf"; the speaker's father's hand, "battered on one knuckle," "with a palm caked hard by dirt" • the speaker's actions: "I hung on like death," "still clinging to your shirt"	• waterlilies: "fill with rain until they overturn, spilling water into water, then rock back, and fill with more"	• the grape sherbet: "his masterpiece," "swirled snow, gelled light," "like salt on a melon," "just how we imagined lavender would taste" • those who have died: "the grassed-over mounds," "we thought no one was lying there under our feet"

SAMPLE PARAGRAPH

The imagery of waterlilies in "I Ask My Mother to Sing" is especially vivid. The speaker describes how the waterlilies floating on a lake in Beijing "fill with rain until they overturn, spilling water into water, then rock back, and fill with more." This image appeals to the sense of sight as well as sound. The descriptions help the reader see and hear the rain as it fills the floating flowers. The image also connects to the mother and grandmother's tears as they remember their homeland so far away.

Setting a Purpose Complete the prereading activity on page 174 and review the teaching options below. Then share with your students what their goals will be, and use these goals to set a purpose for reading. Once students are clear on that purpose, have them write a purpose statement at the top of page 175.

Test Preparation Direct students to read the multiple-choice questions on page 180, as well as the writing prompt on page 181, to help them focus their reading.

LEVEL 1

• Memory

• The Family Memories Project

FOCUS SKILL: Identify Patterns Of Organization

ACTIVITY: SELF-SURVEY

Before assigning the related readings, introduce the survey and have students complete it. Then have partners share their surveys and discuss why some distant memories remain so vivid.

OPTIONS FOR TEACHING

Skill Instruction Use "Learn the Skill" at the bottom of page 174 and page R2 in the Nonfiction Skills Handbook to review the focus skill of identifying patterns of organization.

> **ADDITIONAL RESOURCES:**
>
> **Standards Lesson File: Reading and Informational Texts:** Lesson 2: Sequence and Chronological Order, page 181; Lesson 7: Proposition-and-Support Order, page 227

Jigsaw Learning Divide the class into small groups, each responsible for learning and then sharing information about one of the following topics:
• How our brains process and store memories
• Ways that people compile and preserve memories
If you are using Level 2 in the same classroom, add a third topic about recent research on memory, and use "Messing with Your Mind" as a resource.

Memory Scrapbook Have students interview each other about early childhood or elementary school milestones, and compile a memory scrapbook.

LEVEL 2

• Messing with Your Mind

• Linking Smell and Memory

FOCUS SKILL: Analyze Patterns Of Organization

ACTIVITY: INVESTIGATE

Have students complete the investigation activity outside of class. The following day, have partners share and discuss their completed investigations.

OPTIONS FOR TEACHING

Skill Instruction Use "Learn the Skill" at the bottom of page 174 and page R2 in the Nonfiction Skills Handbook to review the focus skill of analyzing patterns of organization.

> **ADDITIONAL RESOURCES:**
>
> **Standards Lesson File: Reading and Informational Texts:** Lesson 2: Sequence and Chronological Order, page 181; Lesson 7: Proposition-and-Support Order, page 227

Jigsaw Learning Divide the class into small groups, each responsible for answering and then sharing information about one of the following questions:
• How reliable are our memories?
• What triggers help us retain and retrieve memories?
If you are using Level 1 in the classroom, add *How does memory work?* and use "Memory" as a resource.

Perform Memory Tests Present ten ordinary objects to students for about 10 seconds. Then cover the objects. Have students work separately, and then in groups, to make a list of all the objects that they recall seeing.

Memory

Patterns of Organization, page 175
Students should check *main idea and details. Remediation Tip*:
If students mark another choice, review the text and point out
or elicit that the title tells about a general idea, and that all of
the subheadings relate to that main idea.

Specialized Vocabulary, page 176
Students should underline "communicate through thousands
of connections" (line 38). *Remediation Tip*: If necessary, point
out the full definition of synapses and their functions in lines
49–53.

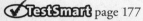 page 177

Answer: D, "all over the cortex"; Students should circle the
subheading *Complete Memories.*

The Family Memories Project

Patterns of Organization, page 178
Students should check *sequential order. Remediation Tip*: If
needed, clarify the difference between chronological order and
sequential order. Remind students that the root word *khronos*
means "time," and the base word *sequence* refers to ordering of
events.

Connect, page 178
Responses will vary but should identify an interview subject
and the information they would like to learn from that person.

Patterns of Organization, page 179
Responses should indicate that *Finally* refers to the last step in
a sequence.

ASSESSMENT PRACTICE II: *p. 180*	
1. A	5. A
2. C	6. C
3. A	7. C
4. D	8. A

Messing with Your Mind

Interpret, page 175
Students may point out that psychologists study and analyze
the workings of the mind and suggest that relating a story from
a psychologist's personal history is an apt lead-in to discussing
how memories are not necessarily exact or objective.

Specialized Vocabulary, page 176
Students should underline clues in lines 30–37 that refer to
research methods of asking questions and quantifying
responses. Definition for *documented*: used formal research
methods

Make Generalizations, page 176
Accept any well-supported response; students will most likely
suggest that memory is not exact and can be shaped by others.

Draw Conclusions, page 177
Responses will likely indicate that since memories are not clear,
complete records, those who interview witnesses should not
place great reliance on the accounts they are given.

Patterns of Organization, page 177
Students may underline "memories can be changed by things
that you are told" (lines 22–23), "But Loftus's research doesn't
stop there" (line 47), "Loftus discusses this idea in a way that's
extremely compelling" (lines 75–76), and "Loftus writes about
some of the reasons" (line 86) and check *proposition and support.*

Linking Smell and Memory

Connect, page 178
Accept any supported response.

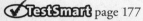 page 179

Answer: C, "main idea and details"; *Remediation Tip*: Some
students may choose "proposition and support"; explain that a
proposition usually argues in favor of an idea that is not likely to
be universally accepted.

ASSESSMENT PRACTICE II: *p. 180*	
1. C	5. D
2. B	6. C
3. B	7. B
4. B	8. C

LEVEL 1

Guide students through the steps described below under Guided Instruction. You may also wish to go over the rubric on the next page. (Consider modifying the rubric for these students, focusing only on Ideas, Organization, and Conventions.) Give students the entire 45 minutes to draft and review their responses. Point out, however, that in an actual timed writing situation, all steps of the writing process must be completed within the given time frame.

LEVEL 2

Share with students the rubric on the next page. Direct them to complete the entire writing process independently, within the actual 45-minute time frame they have been given.

GUIDED INSTRUCTION

ANALYZE THE PROMPT If necessary, lead the students through the three-step analysis process on page 181. Explain that low scores are often the result of the writer missing a critical piece of the directions. The marked prompt should look like this:

Write an essay in which you <u>describe the speaker's view of family memories</u> in one of the poems in this lesson. (How is this view revealed in the poem?) Include (specific examples of) (imagery or figurative language) in your response.

- Point out to students that they should write the name of the poem they will write about on the line provided in part B.
- *Academic Vocabulary*: Clarify for students that they will need to do three things in their **poetry analysis**: describe a speaker's view of family memories, explain how the poem reveals that view, and use examples of imagery or figurative language from the poem that supports their ideas.

PLAN YOUR RESPONSE

- Review with students the steps of a timed writing assignment. For a prompt like this, which requires them to choose one of three poems, and to include examples from the poem they choose, remind them to budget enough time to make a decision, and then locate examples to include. (They should probably spend no more than 10 minutes deciding on a poem and locating examples from it.)
- Students should take time to compose a complete statement about the speaker's view based on details in the chart. Point out that they can use this statement in their essay.
- Students should record exact quotations from the poem in the chart as examples that support their statement about the speaker's view.
- Review the steps under *Organize your information* to help students see that this section provides a clear set of instructions to help them prepare their essay.

WRITE AND REVIEW Encourage students to try out more than one way to open their essay. When they have completed their draft, allow peers to comment on how well the students have met the requirements of the prompt.

RUBRIC FOR TIMED WRITING*

Key Traits	3 (Strong)	2 (Average)	1 (Weak)
IDEAS	• The thesis statement is clear, focused, and compelling. • The analysis is insightful and reveals a deep understanding of the poem. • Relevant details, examples, and quotations from the poem support each key idea.	• The thesis statement is too broad or too narrow. • The analysis shows an adequate understanding of the poem. • Most key ideas are supported by details, examples, and quotations from the poem.	• The thesis statement is unclear or missing. • The analysis consists mostly of a summary. • Details, examples, and quotations from the poem are not relevant or too scarce to support the key ideas.
ORGANIZATION	• The introduction is engaging and clearly presents the topic and the poem to be discussed. • The conclusion summarizes the ideas and draws a conclusion or offers an observation. • Transitional words and phrases show how ideas connect. • The organization is logical and follows essay form.	• The introduction presents the poem to be discussed, but it does not engage the reader. • The conclusion summarizes the ideas but only restates what has been said. • Most of the transitions work, but a few more are needed. • The organization does not follow a consistent pattern.	• The introduction does not clearly set up what the essay is about. • The essay lacks an identifiable conclusion. • The writer uses few, if any, transitional words. • The organization feels random or disjointed; the reader often feels lost or confused.
VOICE	• The tone and voice are appropriate for the purpose and audience. • The writing reflects active engagement with the poem.	• The tone and voice are acceptable but are not strongly individual or direct. • The writing lacks consistent engagement with the poem.	• The voice lacks individuality and is not concerned with or not matched to the audience. • The writing is lifeless or mechanical.
WORD CHOICE	• Words are specific, accurate, and convey precise meaning.	• Words are adequate and mostly correct.	• Limited vocabulary and/or frequent misuse of parts of speech impair understanding.
SENTENCE FLUENCY	• Sentences vary in length and structure. • Sentence beginnings are varied.	• Sentences do not vary in structure. • Some variety of sentence beginnings is attempted.	• Repetitive sentences and fragments occur frequently. • Many sentences begin the same way.
CONVENTIONS	• Spelling, capitalization, and punctuation are correct. • Grammar and usage are correct. • Paragraphing tends to be correct and reinforces the organization.	• Spelling, capitalization, and punctuation are sometimes uneven. • Grammar and usage are not always correct. • Paragraphing is attempted but is not always sound.	• Spelling, capitalization, and punctuation are frequently incorrect. • Grammar and usage mistakes distort meaning. • Paragraphing is missing, irregular, or too frequent.

*Use the Literary Analysis Rubric on the WriteSmart CD if you wish to further modify this chart.

The Seven Ages of Man
by William Shakespeare

The Road Not Taken
by Robert Frost

SUMMARIES:

"The Seven Ages of Man" In this dramatic monologue from *As You Like It,* a character named Jaques describes people as players on the world's stage who go through seven major periods, or "ages in their lives."

"The Road Not Taken" In this metaphorical poem, the speaker describes the choice he made when faced with two roads in a wood. By choosing to go down the less-traveled road, he made a decision that affected the rest of his life.

RELATED NONFICTION:

LEVEL 1

BOOK EXCERPT: from *Choices for the High School Graduate*
In this excerpt, the author argues that while life in the Information Age is vastly different from life during the Industrial Revolution, the questions young people face about their futures have changed very little. (*Readability*: Average)

LEVEL 2

ONLINE ARTICLE: "Who Exactly Is a Grown-Up?"
This article discusses commonly held ideas about when adulthood begins and suggests that these ideas may be shifting in today's world. (*Readability*: Average)

FOCUS AND MOTIVATE *p. 183*

FOR ALL STUDENTS

EXPLORE THE BIG QUESTION: *"Do you set your own COURSE?"*
Discuss the question with students, prompting them to suggest aspects of their lives that they control and parts that are controlled by others. Then have them complete the **Chart It** activity by thinking of personal or professional goals and the steps they would need to follow to reach those goals.

INTRODUCE THE LESSON Tell students that in these selections, they will explore ideas about young people and their futures in today's world. Then call their attention to the Assessment Goals at the bottom of the page.

ASSESSMENT GOALS

LEVEL 1

- identify rhythm, rhyme, and meter in poetry
- use active reading strategies to comprehend text
- evaluate the content of a nonfiction text
- analyze a writing prompt and plan a personal essay

LEVEL 2

- analyze rhythm, rhyme, and meter in poetry
- apply critical thinking skills to analyze text
- evaluate the content of a nonfiction text
- analyze a writing prompt and plan a personal essay

LEVEL 1

Recite familiar nursery rhymes, such as "Jack and Jill" and "Humpty Dumpty" to be certain that students understand basic ideas of **rhythm, rhyme,** and **meter.** Have students tap out the rhythms, note stressed and unstressed syllables, and identify the **rhyme schemes.**

Next, have students suggest examples of verses of popular songs and analyze their rhythm, rhyme, and meter. Finally, remind students that not all poems employ such regular patterns. Explain that poems written in free verse may not include identifiable patterns of rhythm, rhyme, and meter.

LEVEL 2

If helpful, review the definitions of rhythm, rhyme, and meter, and if necessary, provide examples such as those suggested in Level 1, above. You may wish to include these additional points:

- Poets may also use sound devices such as alliteration, assonance, consonance, and repetition to add to a poem's rhythm.

- End rhyme refers to identical or similar sounds that appear at the ends of lines of poetry. Internal rhyme refers to identical or similar sounds that appear within a line of poetry.

- Poems that do not use a regular rhyme scheme may still achieve a natural rhythm.

ADDITIONAL TERMS FOR CRITICAL ANALYSIS

To reinforce understanding of **dramatic monologue** and **symbol,** include the following points in your discussion:

- Identify and discuss other examples of dramatic monologues from Shakespeare's works. Students may be familiar with examples from plays such as *Hamlet, Macbeth,* or *Romeo and Juliet.*

- Symbols appear everywhere, not just in poetry and literature. A flag stands for a country, and the symbols on a flag can represent important national ideas and elements.

ADDITIONAL RESOURCES
from McDougal Littell Literature

STUDENT'S EDITION
Literary Workshop, "The Language of Poetry," p. 668

Additional selection questions, p. 725

STANDARDS LESSON FILE: LITERATURE
Lesson 21: Rhyme and Rhyme Scheme, p. 199

Lesson 22: Rhythm and Meter, p. 207

Lesson 31: Symbol and Symbolism, p. 295

RESOURCE MANAGER
Additional Selection Questions, p. 135

Ideas for Extension, p. 136

Question Support, p. 143

Selection Test A, p. 145

Selection Test B/C, p. 147

BEST PRACTICES TOOLKIT
Evaluating a Poem, p. D17

Core Analysis Frame: Poetry, p. D34

The Seven Ages of Man

CLOSE READ

If you are using this selection primarily for **test preparation**, direct students to preview the multiple choice questions on page 188 and the writing prompt on page 189 to help focus their reading. Explain that this technique may be used any time they take a reading test.

Connect, page 185

Accept reasonable responses that name songs that reveal feelings, thoughts, or hopes. Prompt students to explain how the songs are similar to a dramatic monologue.

Monitor, page 185

Students should mark numbers at the ends of lines as follows:
- 2 at line 8, "school-boy"
- 3 at line 10, "the lover"
- 4 at line 12, "a soldier"
- 5 at line 16, "the justice"

Clarify, page 186

Students should mark a regular pattern of stressed and unstressed syllables in lines 26–29. *Remediation Tip*: If students are uncertain of the pattern, have them read the lines aloud slowly and tap out the rhythm. Then have them mark just the stressed syllables.

Pause & Reflect, page 186

MAKE JUDGMENTS Accept reasoned, supported responses. Those who feel the attitude is gloomy may cite the negative connotations of words such *childishness* and *oblivion*. Students who find the attitude realistic may point out that many elderly people experience the conditions the speaker describes.

The Road Not Taken

Analyze, page 187

Students should mark the rhyme scheme as follows: line 4, *a*; line 5, *b*; line 6, *c*; line 7, *d*; line 8, *c*; line 9, *c*; line 10, *d*.

✓TestSmart page 187

Answer: C, "eight"; Remediation Tip: If students mark *B*, four, remind them to read the question carefully and note that it asks about the total number of stressed syllables in lines 11–12.

Pause & Reflect, page 187

INTERPRET Students should mark "a life that is not ordinary."

ASSESSMENT PRACTICE I: *p. 188*	
1. B	5. C
2. C	6. D
3. B	7. C
4. A	8. D
Point out to students that the test-taking strategies they learned as they read can be used with the following item: • Item 7: tap out stressed syllables (page 187)	

The Seven Ages of Man

SECOND READ: CRITICAL ANALYSIS

If you are using this selection primarily for **test preparation**, direct students to preview the multiple choice questions on page 188 and the writing prompt on page 189 to help focus their reading. Explain that this technique may be used any time they take a reading test.

Draw Conclusions, page 185

Students may underline the following: "Mewling and puking" (line 7), "whining" (line 8), "Sighing like furnace" (line 11), "bubble reputation" (line 15). Adjectives that could describe the speaker's outlook include *gloomy, pessimistic,* and *cynical,* but accept all reasonable responses.

✓TestSmart page 186

Answer: C, "five"; Remediation Tip: Point out that stressed syllables often fall on words that are important; in line 20, the most important words are *so, plays, part, sixth,* and *shifts.*

Analyze, page 186

No; with the exception of lines 22–23, the poem does not use end rhymes.

The Road Not Taken

Interpret, page 187

Students should circle "Two roads diverged in a yellow wood" (line 1). Responses should indicate that the image represents two choices.

Analyze, page 187

Students should mark the rhyme scheme for the final stanza as *abaab,* and should mark a regular pattern of stressed and unstressed syllables. *Remediation Tip*: If students are uncertain of the pattern, have them read the lines aloud slowly and tap out the rhythm. Then have them mark just the stressed syllables.

ASSESSMENT PRACTICE I: *p. 188*	
1. B	5. A
2. C	6. D
3. B	7. C
4. A	8. D
Point out to students that the test-taking strategies they learned as they read can be used with the following item: • Item 7: tap out stressed syllables (page 186)	

SHORT RESPONSE: PARAGRAPH Use this writing activity to determine whether students understand the use of rhyme and rhythm in poetry. Take them through the following steps:

- Have students analyze the prompt. They should notice that they are being asked to write a paragraph about how rhyme and rhythm are used in one of the poems they have read.

- Have them complete the graphic organizer. Point out that they can write general statements describing the rhyme and rhythm in the first column, and write examples from the poem that illustrate the statements in the second column.

- Explain that they can then write their paragraph using their ideas from the organizer, but they will also need to include ideas about how rhythm and rhyme affect the poem and its message.

TEST-TAKER'S TOOLKIT

Poem Title: *"The Road Not Taken"*

Examples from the Poem

Rhyme	Rhythm

Regular rhyme scheme of abaab
 	
    wood (line 1), stood (line 3), could (line 4)
 	
    both (line 2), undergrowth (line 5)
	Regular pattern of stressed and unstressed syllables, stress falling on important words
	Steady rhythm, much like walking
	
	    Line 1: Two roads diverged in a yellow wood
	
	    Line 20: And that has made all the difference

SAMPLE PARAGRAPH

Robert Frost uses rhythm and rhyme to great effect in his poem "The Road Not Taken." A clear rhyme scheme is evident throughout the poem. For example, in the first stanza, the rhyme scheme is abaab. The first, third, and fourth lines use the end rhymes wood, stood, and could. The second and fifth lines use the end rhymes both and undergrowth. The poem uses a regular rhythmic pattern of stressed and unstressed syllables, with the stresses falling on important words, such as in the last line, "And that has made all the difference." The regular patterns of rhythm and rhyme resemble a walking beat; they serve to keep the thoughts moving at a steady pace and to support the poet's ideas.

SETTING A PURPOSE Complete the prereading activity on page 190 and review the teaching options below. Then share with your students what their goals will be, and use these goals to set a purpose for reading. Once students are clear on that purpose, have them write a purpose statement at the top of page 191.

TEST PREPARATION Direct students to read the multiple-choice questions on page 194, as well as the writing prompt on page 195, to help them focus their reading.

<table>
<tr><td>

LEVEL 1

• from *Choices for the High School Graduate*

FOCUS SKILL: EVALUATE CONTENT

ACTIVITY: SELF-SURVEY

Before assigning the related readings, introduce the survey on page 190 and have students complete it. Then have partners share their surveys and discuss how their ideas are similar and different.

OPTIONS FOR TEACHING

SKILL INSTRUCTION Use "Learn the Skill" at the bottom of page 190 and page R2 in the Nonfiction Skills Handbook to review the focus skill of evaluating content.

> **ADDITIONAL RESOURCES:**
> **STANDARDS LESSON FILE: READING AND INFORMATIONAL TEXTS:** Lesson 16: Evaluating Content, page 317

DISCUSSION Divide the class into small groups and use the following questions to guide their discussion:

- Do you agree that people in the nineteenth century had far fewer choices about work than we do today?
- What would Jaques have to say about the nonfiction selection you read?
- Which insight or piece of advice from the nonfiction selection did you find most compelling? Why?

If you are using Level 2 in the same classroom, have mixed groups briefly describe and summarize the texts they have read before they begin their discussion.

INTERVIEW Have students interview their parents, or other older relatives about how they made choices about work and careers during their lifetimes. Then have small groups share their interviews.

</td><td>

LEVEL 2

• Who Exactly Is a Grown-Up?

FOCUS SKILL: EVALUATE CONTENT

ACTIVITY: SELF-SURVEY

Before assigning the related readings, introduce the survey on page 190 and have students complete it. Then have partners share their surveys and discuss how their ideas are similar and different.

OPTIONS FOR TEACHING

SKILL INSTRUCTION Use "Learn the Skill" at the bottom of page 190 and page R2 in the Nonfiction Skills Handbook to review the focus skill of evaluating content.

> **ADDITIONAL RESOURCES:**
> **STANDARDS LESSON FILE: READING AND INFORMATIONAL TEXT:** Lesson 16: Evaluating Content, page 317

DISCUSSION Divide the class into small groups and use the following questions to guide their discussion:

- Do you agree that ideas about adulthood are shifting in today's world? Why or why not?
- Which idea from the nonfiction selection surprised you most? Why?
- To which poem or piece of nonfiction did you most relate? Why?

If you are using Level 1 in the same classroom, have mixed groups briefly describe and summarize the text they have read before they begin their discussion.

POETIC RESPONSE Have partners or small groups work together to write a humorous poem about stages or choices in today's world in the form of either "The Seven Ages of Man" or "The Road Not Taken." Invite students to present their poems to the class.

</td></tr>
</table>

from *Choices for the High School Graduate*

Evaluate Content, page 191
Accept reasonable, supported responses. Some students may find the generalization makes them more skeptical about the author's ideas; others may see the generalization as just a lead-in to her ideas, and thus may not see it as too intrusive.

Specialized Vocabulary, page 192
Students should underline "Information Age" (line 13). The label suggests that increased access to information is important in today's world.

Evaluate Content, page 192
Students should check the third choice, "a high school senior . . . after graduating"; *Remediation Tip*: If students check a different choice, ask them to explain their choice. Point out that the selection does not discuss particular careers and that the author's purpose is not primarily to entertain, but to inform readers about how choices have changed over time.

TestSmart page 193
Answer: C, "there is no one right choice . . . "; Students should underline "Doug wanted to quit . . . find out who I was'" (lines 46–47), "She was ready . . . sixteenth birthday" (line 50), and "After a painful . . . take time out" (lines 54–56).

Evaluate Content, page 193
Accept all supported responses. Students will most likely suggest that the excerpt provides a fairly accurate idea of the many choices that teenagers face today and cite personal or commonly known experiences as support.

ASSESSMENT PRACTICE II: *p. 194*	
1. D	5. B
2. A	6. C
3. C	7. D
4. C	8. A

Who Exactly Is a Grown-Up?

Evaluate Content, page 191
Possible response: Some college graduates find that they are still waiting to become "real adults." Facts students might identify include "She is 22 . . . living in her parents' suburban home" (lines 10–11). Opinions could include either sentence in lines 14–17.

TestSmart page 192
Answer: C, " . . . marriage and children are marks of adulthood."
Remediation Tip: Point out that information from the survey appears in two different paragraphs. Have students scan the text to find information about results from the survey that match the correct answer choice.

Evaluate Content, page 192
Students should mark a *1* by the anecdote about Daniel Gluck (lines 34–38), and a 2 by the anecdote about Ashley Mohney (lines 41–46). Responses about whether the anecdotes support the text's ideas may vary in degree but will likely suggest that they support the author's ideas.

Specialized Vocabulary, page 193
Students may underline "notion of delayed adulthood" (line 67), "30 is the new 20" (line 68), and "40 is the new 30" (lines 68–69), and should indicate that *ripple effect* means something that happens as a result of something else happening.

Evaluate Content, page 193
Accept all reasoned, supported responses.

ASSESSMENT PRACTICE II: *p. 194*	
1. A	5. C
2. B	6. B
3. D	7. D
4. B	8. A

LEVEL 1

Guide students through the steps described below under Guided Instruction. You may also wish to go over the rubric on the next page. (Consider modifying the rubric for these students, focusing only on Ideas, Organization, and Conventions.) Give students the entire 30 minutes to draft and review their responses. Point out, however, that in an actual timed writing situation, all steps of the writing process must be completed within the given time frame.

LEVEL 2

Share with students the rubric on the next page. Direct them to complete the entire writing process independently, within the actual 30-minute time frame they have been given.

GUIDED INSTRUCTION

ANALYZE THE PROMPT If necessary, lead students through the two-step analysis process on page 195. Explain that low scores are often the result of the writer missing a critical piece of the directions. The marked prompt should look like this:

> If preparing for adulthood is like getting ready to go on a long journey, what do you want to take with you on your trip? Write a (personal essay) in which you describe three "things"— objects, resources, or ideas—you will need to become an adult, as well as why you need these things. Support your ideas with examples from your own life.

- *Academic Vocabulary*: Point out that a **personal essay** is one in which the author expresses his or her thoughts and feelings about a subject. Explain that while there are no right or wrong responses, students will need to clearly describe and support their ideas.
- Clarify for students that their essays should not consist of general ideas about what people need to become adults, but should focus on their own lives and futures.

Remind students that all the elements in the text they underlined have to be addressed in their responses if they want to achieve the highest score on the test.

PLAN YOUR RESPONSE
- Review with students the steps of a timed writing assignment. For a prompt like this, which requires them to explain three things they will need to become an adult, remind them to budget enough time to think about, list, and select or refine their ideas. (They should probably spend no more than 5–10 minutes brainstorming and selecting ideas.)
- Review the steps under *Organize your information* to help students see that this section provides a clear set of instructions to help them prepare their essay.

WRITE AND REVIEW Encourage students to develop the image of a journey in the opening of their essay (using peer feedback to choose the most effective if time allows). When they have completed their draft, allow peers to comment on how well the students have met the requirements of the prompt.

RUBRIC FOR TIMED WRITING*

KEY TRAITS	3 (STRONG)	2 (AVERAGE)	1 (WEAK)
IDEAS	• The writer focuses on his or her thoughts and feelings about a subject. • Vivid and relevant details support the writer's ideas.	• For the most part, the writer focuses on the subject. • Relevant details support ideas, but a few more are needed.	• Thoughts and feelings are not well defined. • Details and examples are mostly unrelated and wandering.
ORGANIZATION	• The introduction clearly focuses on the writer's life and future and draws the reader in. • The conclusion summarizes the writer's thoughts and draws a conclusion or offers an observation. • Transitional words and phrases clearly show how ideas connect. • The organization is logical and follows a consistent pattern.	• The introduction focuses on the writer's life, but it does not draw the reader in. • The conclusion summarizes the writer's thoughts but only restates what has been said. • Most of the transitions show how ideas connect, but a few more are needed. • The organization shows some logic but does not follow a consistent pattern.	• The introduction does not clearly set up what the essay is about. • The essay lacks an identifiable conclusion. • The writer uses few, if any, transitional words to connect ideas. • The organization feels random or disjointed; the reader often feels lost or confused.
VOICE	• The tone and voice reflect the writer's personality and are appropriate for the purpose and audience. • The writing reflects active engagement with the topic.	• The tone and voice are acceptable for the purpose and audience but do not reflect the writer's personality. • The writing lacks consistent engagement with the topic.	• The voice lacks individuality and is not concerned with or not matched to the audience. • The writing is lifeless or mechanical.
WORD CHOICE	• Words are specific, accurate and convey a precise meaning.	• Words are adequate and mostly correct.	• Limited vocabulary and/or frequent misuse of parts of speech impair understanding.
SENTENCE FLUENCY	• Sentences vary in length and structure. • Sentence beginnings are varied.	• Sentences do not significantly vary in structure. • Some variety of sentence beginnings is attempted.	• Repetitive sentence structure, fragments, and run-on sentences make the writing difficult to follow. • Many sentences begin the same way.
CONVENTIONS	• Spelling, capitalization, and punctuation are generally correct. • Grammar and usage are correct. • Paragraphing tends to be correct and reinforces the organization.	• Spelling, capitalization, and punctuation are sometimes uneven. • Grammar and usage are not always correct. • Paragraphing is attempted but is not always sound.	• Spelling, capitalization, and punctuation are frequently incorrect. • Grammar and usage mistakes are frequent and distort meaning. • Paragraphing is missing, irregular, or too frequent.

*Use the Autobiographical Narrative Rubric on the WriteSmart CD if you wish to further modify this chart.

Where Have You Gone, Charming Billy?

by Tim O'Brien

SUMMARY:

In this short story about the war in Vietnam, Private First Class Paul Berlin and his unit head toward the sea, where they hope to find safety. During the journey, he reflects on an event from earlier in the day when fellow soldier Billy Boy Watkins became so terrified after stepping on a mine that he died of a heart attack.

RELATED NONFICTION:

LEVEL 1

TIMELINE: "U.S. Involvement in Vietnam"
This timeline shows national and international events before, during, and after the Vietnam War. (*Readability*: Easy)

TEXTBOOK EXCERPT: "A Different Kind of War"
This excerpt explores the unique obstacles American soldiers faced in Vietnam. (*Readability*: Average)

LEVEL 2

ENCYCLOPEDIA ENTRY: "Post-Traumatic Stress Disorder"
The psychological difficulties that can follow a traumatic event are described in this encyclopedia entry. (*Readability*: Challenging)

ONLINE ARTICLE: "Combat Stress: The War Within"
This article discusses the psychological and emotional damage that affects some soldiers who fought in Iraq and Afghanistan. (*Readability*: Average)

FOCUS AND MOTIVATE *p. 197*

FOR ALL STUDENTS

EXPLORE THE BIG QUESTION: *"Is FEAR our worst enemy?"*
Discuss the question with students, asking them to name stories and movies that include characters who experience fear. Encourage students to tell how these characters behave while in the throes of fear. Then have them complete the **Discuss It** activity with a partner.

INTRODUCE THE LESSON Tell students that in these selections, they will explore ideas about wars, how some have been fought, and how combat affects soldiers. Students in Level 1 will read two additional selections about the Vietnam War. Students in Level 2 will read two selections that describe how traumatic events affect mental health. Then call their attention to the Assessment Goals at the bottom of the page.

ASSESSMENT GOALS

LEVEL 1

- analyze the author's style and voice in a work of fiction
- use active reading strategies to comprehend text
- paraphrase and summarize ideas in works of nonfiction
- analyze a writing prompt and plan a personal narrative

LEVEL 2

- analyze the author's style and voice in a work of fiction
- apply critical thinking skills to analyze text
- synthesize information from fiction and nonfiction text
- analyze a writing prompt and plan a personal narrative

LEVEL 1

To help students analyze an **author's style** and **voice,** have partners work together to write a few sentences on one or more general topics, like those suggested below. Hand each pair a slip of paper that assigns them a style—formal, informal, journalistic, or literary—to use in writing their sentences. Some general topics could include:

- an extreme weather event
- a going-away party
- the sighting of an unusual animal in a town
- a new technological device

When the pairs have completed their sentences, read them aloud, one at a time. Ask students to determine which style is used in each case. Discuss their responses, and how they analyzed each author's style and voice.

LEVEL 2

If helpful, review the definitions of author's style and voice. You may wish to include these additional points:

- An author's choice of words—and their connotations—can shape the voice readers hear.
- The sentence structure an author employs can also shape style and voice. Short, simple sentences may be used to express ideas in a direct way. Longer, more complex sentences may be used to connect complicated ideas.
- Word choice and details can be used to create a specific tone that helps reveal the author's attitude toward his or her topic.

ADDITIONAL TERMS FOR CRITICAL ANALYSIS

To reinforce understanding of **flashback** and **realism,** have students give examples of texts and movies that incorporate these elements and discuss their uses and effectiveness. Have students ask themselves the following questions as they read "Where Have You Gone, Charming Billy?":

- How would the story be different if the author had not used flashback but had presented the events in chronological order?
- What features of realism does the author use? What effect does the use of realism have on the story and its readers?

ADDITIONAL RESOURCES
from **McDougal Littell Literature**

STUDENT'S EDITION
Literary Workshop, "Author's Style and Voice," p. 774

Additional selection questions, p. 761

STANDARDS LESSON FILE: LITERATURE
Lesson 8: Foreshadowing and Flashback, p. 69

Lesson 46: Style and Syntax, p. 437

RESOURCE MANAGER
Selection Summary, pp. 25, 26

Additional Selection Questions, p. 21

Ideas for Extension, p. 22

Vocabulary Study, p. 31

Vocabulary in Context, p. 32

Reading Check, p. 34

Question Support, p. 35

Selection Test A, p. 39

Selection Test B/C, p. 41

BEST PRACTICES TOOLKIT
Author's Craft, p. D24

VOCABULARY IN CONTEXT Read aloud the context phrases below and show students how to use context clues to figure out meaning. Once students have offered their own suggestions, review the actual definitions.

SELECTION VOCABULARY

stealth *(n.)*: cautious or secret action or movement (line 7)
fecund *(adj.)*: producing much growth; fertile (line 45)
diffuse *(adj.)*: unfocused (line 59)
inertia *(n.)*: tendency to continue to do what one has been doing (line 124)

CONTEXT PHRASES

1. the use of **stealth** to remain undetected

2. a huge harvest from the fertile, **fecund** fields

3. difficult to identify one smell in the mix of **diffuse** scents

4. the **inertia** of relaxing on a hot summer day

Idioms Make sure students are familiar with the following expressions that appear in this story.

- **a boogieman in the closet** (line 60): a childish fear of shapes in the dark
- **get used to it** (line 151): become accustomed to something unfamiliar or unpleasant
- **did not matter much** (line 157): wasn't very important
- **croaking** (line 177): dying

Where Have You Gone, Charming Billy?

CLOSE READ

If you are using this selection primarily for **test preparation**, direct students to preview the multiple choice questions on page 207 and the writing prompt on page 208 to help focus their reading. Explain that this technique may be used any time they take a reading test.

Make Inferences, page 199

Students should circle words and phrases such as "not talking" (line 2), "quietly" (lines 4, 12), "motioning with his hand" (line 5), "stealth" (line 7), "they did not move" (line 7), and "Except for the sounds of their breathing" (lines 7–8). Responses should indicate that the soldiers are probably being silent because they are in a dangerous area or situation.

Analyze, page 200

Students should circle lines of dialogue that seem realistic, such as lines 29–32, which include features such as short, clipped statements, italics for emphasis, and common conversational expressions such as "Hey!" and "Okay." *Remediation Tip*: Have partners read the dialogue aloud to hear its natural and believable quality.

Analyze, page 200

Students should check the third choice, *both*. They may note that this choice allows the author to use short sentences to present Paul's thoughts and feelings and use longer sentences to describe events and the physical environment.

Pause & Reflect, page 201

1. *CLARIFY* Students should indicate that these activities help keep his mind off unpleasant thoughts. *Remediation Tip*: Point out that the sentence in line 70 provides a clue: "There were tricks he'd learned to keep from thinking."
2. *MAKE INFERENCES* Students will likely infer that Paul looks to his father for comfort and approval. *Remediation Tip*: If students have difficulty forming an inference, have them combine their own knowledge about fathers and sons with clues the author has provided so far about Paul and his father.

✓TestSmart page 202

Answer: C, "the dog could alert the villagers . . ."

Monitor, page 202

Students might circle sensory details such as the following: smells ("straw, cattle, mildew") and sounds ("barking died away") in lines 99–102; sight ("conical-shaped burial mounds") and smells ("perfumy smell") in lines 103–104; visual details ("face turning pale and the veins popping out") in lines 115–116 and in lines 119–125.

Analyze, page 203

Accept any supported response. Some students might suggest that they hear the voice of the writer; others may hear the voice of Paul Berlin. Because O'Brien weaves his voice with Paul's thoughts and descriptions, it is possible to hear Paul's voice *and* the writer's voice.

Predict, page 203

Accept any supported response. Most will likely suggest that the conversation with Toby will make Paul feel less fearful.

Pause & Reflect, page 204

1. *DRAW CONCLUSIONS* Students should underline clues related to Toby's actions, such as making conversation, offering to share gum and giving advice to point out the differences between the characters. They may cite his aura of calm and confidence.
2. *MAKE INFERENCES* Students may suggest that because he is more experienced, Toby knows that popping bubbles could attract unwanted attention.

Make Judgments, page 205

Students will likely mark *yes*. They are likely to point out that people can have extreme reactions to deep fear and that Paul's giggling is a form of hysteria. *Remediation Tip*: Point out lines 219–220, in which the narrator notes how Paul's giggling is much like Billy Boy's bawling.

✓TestSmart Vocabulary, page 205

Answer: A, "carried out"

Pause & Reflect, page 206

1. *CLARIFY* Students might suggest that the soldier smothers Paul to quiet him so that the noise doesn't put them in danger and to try to calm Paul down.
2. *COMPARE* They can both be hysterical reactions to extreme fear.

Big Question page 206

Most students will point out that the story's closing line shows that Paul is not successful at combating his fear. *Remediation Tip*: If students are unsure, have them trace the strategies Paul uses to take his mind off his fear, such as counting, imagining a more pleasant scene or event, and singing. Then discuss how they did not work, since Paul later becomes hysterical with giggles and cannot control himself.

ASSESSMENT PRACTICE I: *p. 207*	
1. A	5. D
2. B	6. D
3. D	7. C
4. A	8. A

Point out to students that the test-taking strategies they learned as they read can be used with the following items:
- Item 2: use prior knowledge (page 202)
- Items 7, 8: substitute answer choices (page 205)

Where Have You Gone, Charming Billy?

SECOND READ: CRITICAL ANALYSIS

If you are using this selection primarily for **test preparation**, direct students to preview the multiple choice questions on page 207 and the writing prompt on page 208 to help focus their reading. Explain that this technique may be used any time they take a reading test.

Analyze, page 199

Accept all reasonable responses. Students may say that O'Brien's use of long and short sentences helps the reader understand both simple and complex ideas; that this technique enhances the realism and helps the reader identify with Paul, who like many readers, does not fully comprehend the circumstances of fighting in a war.

Identify, page 200

Accept any supported response. Some students might suggest that they hear the voice of the writer; others may hear the voice of Paul Berlin. Some may point out that because O'Brien weaves his voice with Paul's thoughts and descriptions, it is possible to hear Paul's voice *and* the writer's voice.

Analyze, page 200

The dialogue in the boxed text is informal and realistic. Students may circle common interjections and expressions such as "Hey!" (line 29) and "Okay" (line 30), and informal statements such as "if I thought you was sleepin'" (line 35).

Draw Conclusions, page 201

Students will likely suggest that Paul's song suggests that he is wishing for the safety and security of home and his mother's care.

✔TestSmart, page 202

Answer: C, "the dog could alert the villagers . . ."

Analyze, page 202

Students might underline details that describe smells and sounds in lines 99–102, sight and smells in lines 103–104, visual details in lines 115–116 and 119–125. They should note that these details give the reader the sense of being in Paul's place—of being able to experience what he is seeing and feeling.

Analyze, page 203

Responses may indicate that using his full military title serves as a reminder that war and military service are serious and that Paul is no longer just Paul Berlin—he is a soldier, first and foremost.

Draw Conclusions, page 203

Students are likely to suggest that Paul's feelings are typical, and may underline "They been fighting wars a long time, and you get used to it" (lines 151–152). Accept all supported responses.

Interpret, page 204

Responses may indicate that Paul's greatest fear is that he is a coward and that he will be seen as a coward by others, especially by his father.

✔TestSmart Vocabulary, page 205

Answer: C, "stop or repress"

Evaluate, page 205

Most students are likely to indicate that withholding the details of Billy Boy's death is effective, as not knowing keeps the reader interested in—and increasingly apprehensive about—what happened to Billy Boy. *Remediation Tip*: If students suggest that this stylistic choice is not effective, ask them to explain their response. Discuss how effective or interesting the story would be if O'Brien had presented the details of Billy Boy's death early in the story.

Compare, page 206

Both laughter and crying are emotional responses that can be uncontrollable; both can be hysterical reactions to extreme fear.

Big Question 2, page 206

Most students will probably point out that the story's closing line shows that Paul is not successful at combating his fear. *Remediation Tip*: If students are unsure, have them trace the strategies Paul uses to take his mind off his fear, such as counting, imagining a more pleasant scene or event, and singing. Then discuss how they did not work, since Paul later becomes hysterical with giggles and cannot control himself.

ASSESSMENT PRACTICE I: *p. 207*	
1. B	5. D
2. D	6. D
3. C	7. C
4. A	8. A

Point out to students that the test-taking strategies they learned as they read can be used with the following items:
- Item 1: use prior knowledge (page 202)
- Items 7, 8: substitute answer choices (page 205)

SHORT RESPONSE: PARAGRAPH Use this writing activity to determine whether students can identify and understand stylistic elements in a work of fiction. Take them through the following steps:

- Have students analyze the prompt. They should notice that they are being asked to write one or two paragraphs.
- Review the stylistic elements listed under *Academic Vocabulary*. Then have them complete the chart. Point out that they should list the three elements that they think are the strongest factors in the author's style.
- Explain that they can list more than one example for each stylistic element, but that they should include the strongest example in their paragraphs.

TEST-TAKER'S TOOLKIT

STYLISTIC ELEMENTS	EXAMPLES
sensory details	silence in lines 4–17 smells and touch in lines 42–45 sights and smells in lines 99–104
sentence structure	long and short sentences used in lines 37–46, 51–66
voice	informal, as in dialogue in lines 27–35, 135–145

SAMPLE PARAGRAPH

In "Where Have You Gone, Charming Billy?" Tim O'Brien uses stylistic elements such as sensory details, sentence structure, and voice to make the story realistic. In the opening of the story, O'Brien vividly describes the sights and silence as Private First Class Paul Berlin and his unit move at night toward the sea. The soldiers squat "in the shadows, vanishing in the primitive stealth of warfare"; they are silent "(e)xcept for the sounds of their breathing." O'Brien's combination of short and long sentences also adds to the realism. In lines 51–66, short sentences describe Paul's plans about the next morning; one long sentence combines complex ideas about these plans and Paul's deep fear of being afraid. Finally, O'Brien's use of informal language in dialogue adds to the story's realism. The short, clipped sentences in lines 135–145 use slang, contractions, and everyday expressions to great effect as they realistically reveal two young men who are strangers to one another but know that they share a common, if unpleasant, bond.

Setting a Purpose Complete the prereading activity on page 209 and review the teaching options below. Then share with your students what their goals will be, and use these goals to set a purpose for reading. Once students are clear on that purpose, have them write a purpose statement at the top of page 210.

Test Preparation Direct students to read the multiple-choice questions on page 214, as well as the writing prompt on page 215, to help them focus their reading.

LEVEL 1

- **U.S. Involvement in Vietnam**
- **A Different Kind of War**

FOCUS SKILL: Summarize and Paraphrase

ACTIVITY: BROADEN YOUR KNOWLEDGE

Have students complete the first two columns of the K-W-L chart the day before you assign the reading. Have them fill out the third column after reading.

OPTIONS FOR TEACHING

Skill Instruction Use "Learn the Skill" at the bottom of page 209 and page R2 in the Nonfiction Skills Handbook to review the focus skill of summarizing and paraphrasing.

> **ADDITIONAL RESOURCES:**
>
> **Standards Lesson File:** Reading and Informational Texts: Lesson 4: Recognizing Main Idea and Details, page 33

Jigsaw Learning Divide the class into small groups, each responsible for learning and then sharing information about one of the following topics:
- causes and events of the Vietnam War
- military strategies used by the Viet Cong and the United States

If you are using Level 2 in the same classroom, add a topic about the toll of war on soldiers' mental health and use "Post-Traumatic Stress Disorder" as a resource.

Interview Have small groups of students contact a local association for Vietnam veterans and arrange to interview one or more veterans about the experience of fighting in Vietnam. Then have students prepare questions for their interviews, and later tell the class about their interviews.

LEVEL 2

- **Post-Traumatic Stress Disorder**
- **Combat Stress: The War Within**

FOCUS SKILL: Synthesize Information

ACTIVITY: ASSESS YOUR KNOWLEDGE

Have students complete the left column of the chart before you assign the reading. Have them complete the right column of the chart after reading.

OPTIONS FOR TEACHING

Skill Instruction Use "Learn the Skill" at the bottom of page 209 and page R2 in the Nonfiction Skills Handbook to review the focus skill of synthesizing information.

> **ADDITIONAL RESOURCES:**
>
> **Standards Lesson File:** Reading and Informational Texts: Lesson 14: Synthesizing Information, page 133

Jigsaw Learning Divide the class into small groups, each responsible for learning and then sharing information about one of the following topics:
- causes and effects of post-traumatic stress disorder
- studies on the mental health of combat troops

If you are using Level 1 in the same classroom, add a topic about the unique challenges soldiers in Vietnam faced and use "A Different Kind of War" as a resource.

Investigation Have small groups work together to investigate local mental health organizations, therapists, and veterans' support groups to learn what services are available to veterans of war in their area. Have each group present their findings to the class.

U.S. Involvement in Vietnam

Paraphrase, page 210
Possible response: France's takeover of Vietnam's government in 1858 eventually led to the Vietnam War. In response to the struggles against this foreign rule, a Communist movement developed in Vietnam. At the same time, the United States was working to stop the spread of communism. *Remediation Tip*: Have students read each sentence, stop, and then use their own words to orally restate and simplify the main ideas.

A Different Kind of War

Paraphrase, page 211
Student's paraphrases should include simplified main ideas: Every war is different. In World War II, powerful new weapons were used. Extreme weather and climate conditions made the Korean War unique. The Vietnam War brought new challenges.

Draw Conclusions, page 211
Students should check the first choice, "It gave the Viet Cong the element of surprise. . . ." Students should underline clues in lines 19–21 that describe the advantages guerilla warfare gave the Viet Cong.

Make Inferences, page 212
Students will likely infer that soldiers under constant stress would lose confidence and focus, leading them to make poor decisions that would cause harm.

Specialized Vocabulary, page 212
Students should underline "the mental or emotional state of a group" (line 50). Students' sentences should reflect their understanding of *morale* and the story's situation. Sample sentence: *The soldiers in the story suffered from low morale as they faced difficult conditions and saw a fellow soldier die.*

Summarize, page 213
Factors affecting morale included constant stress and being drafted to fight in a war that many people opposed. Accept any supported response to determine which factor would have been hardest for soldiers to deal with.

✓TestSmart page 213
Answer: C, "booby traps"; *Remediation Tip*: If students mark another choice, ask them to explain their choice. Have them return to lines 82–88 and note the descriptions of many kinds of traps.

ASSESSMENT PRACTICE II: *p. 214*	
1. C	5. D
2. B	6. C
3. A	7. A
4. B	8. D

Post-Traumatic Stress Disorder

Synthesize, page 210
Students will probably conclude that soldiers in Vietnam were at a high risk of developing PTSD because of the many traumatic events and constant anxiety. *Remediation Tip*: If students think that soldiers in Vietnam were unlikely to develop PTSD, discuss the events described in "Where Have You Gone, Charming Billy?"—particularly those details surrounding the death of Billy Boy Watkins—to help them understand the trauma of the situation.

✓TestSmart page 210
Answer: D, "reactions"; *Remediation Tip*: If students mark another choice, have them review the Tip and reread lines 29–36 carefully.

Synthesize, page 211
Accept any reasonable, supported response. Students may suggest that Sergeant Facto and Paul Berlin go through similar emotional changes, but these changes manifest themselves differently for each man.

Infer and Make Judgments, page 212
Possible consequences of freezing up while on patrol might include not fulfilling his duties and bringing harm to himself and possibly many others. Students will likely conclude that Facto did not show cowardice, but accept all reasonable, supported responses.

Synthesize, page 212
Accept all responses that indicate that students are able to bring together information from a number of sources to form new or deeper ideas.

Synthesize, page 213
Students should recognize that not getting treatment for PTSD could have many negative long-term consequences for officers and the soldiers that serve under their command, and that these factors could seriously affect their careers.

ASSESSMENT PRACTICE II: *p. 214*	
1. C	5. D
2. A	6. C
3. B	7. A
4. C	8. B

LEVEL 1

Guide students through the steps described below under Guided Instruction. You may also wish to go over the rubric on the next page. (Consider modifying the rubric for these students, focusing only on Ideas, Organization, and Conventions.) Give students the entire 45 minutes to draft and review their responses. Point out, however, that in an actual timed writing situation, all steps of the writing process must be completed within the given time frame.

LEVEL 2

Share with students the rubric on the next page. Direct them to complete the entire writing process independently, within the actual 45-minute time frame they have been given.

GUIDED INSTRUCTION

ANALYZE THE PROMPT If necessary, lead students through the two-step analysis process on page 215. Explain that low scores are often the result of the writer missing a critical piece of the directions. The marked prompt should look like this:

> The soldier in "Where Have You Gone, Charming Billy?" has to overcome his fear to survive. <u>When have you had to face and overcome fears?</u> Write a <u>personal narrative</u> in which you ⟨share a frightening experience⟩. As you ⟨describe the events⟩, ⟨choose vivid words⟩ that will help your readers feel as if they were there with you.

- *Academic Vocabulary*: Point out that a **personal narrative** is a story from the author's own life. Explain to students that they will be the main character in the story and should use the pronoun *I*.
- Clarify for students that their narratives do not have to be about a truly terrifying event— many people have to face their fears when they learn to ride a bike or take an airplane trip. Students should not disclose any information they feel uncomfortable about sharing.

PLAN YOUR RESPONSE

- Review with students the steps of a timed writing assignment. For a prompt like this, which requires them to write a short narrative, remind them to budget enough time to think about, plan, and write the narrative. (They should probably spend no more than 10–15 minutes choosing an event and planning their writing.)
- Students should use the chart to jot down notes for their narrative's exposition, rising action, climax, falling action, and resolution. They can use their notes as an outline when they write their narratives.

WRITE AND REVIEW Encourage students to try several different openings. When they have completed their draft, allow peers to comment on how well the students have met the requirements of the prompt.

RUBRIC FOR TIMED WRITING*

KEY TRAITS	3 (STRONG)	2 (AVERAGE)	1 (WEAK)
IDEAS	• The writing focuses on a compelling, well-defined experience. • Vivid and relevant details re-create the experience. • Dialogue is relevant and engaging.	• The writing focuses on a well-defined experience. • Relevant details re-create the experience, but more are needed. • Dialogue is relevant.	• The experience is not well defined. • Details and examples are mostly unrelated and wandering. • Dialogue is rarely present.
ORGANIZATION	• The introduction clearly presents the experience and draws the reader in. • The conclusion summarizes the experience and draws a conclusion or offers an observation. • Transitional words and phrases clearly show the order of events. • The organization is logical and follows a consistent pattern.	• The introduction presents the experience, but it does not draw the reader in. • The conclusion summarizes the experience but only restates what has been said. • Most of the transitions show the order of events, but a few more are needed. • The organization shows some logic but does not follow a consistent pattern.	• The introduction does not clearly set up what the narrative is about. • The narrative lacks an identifiable conclusion. • The writer uses few, if any, transitional words to show the order of events. • The organization feels random or disjointed; the reader often feels lost or confused.
VOICE	• The tone and voice reflect the writer's personality and are appropriate for the purpose and audience. • The writing reflects active engagement with the topic.	• The tone and voice are acceptable but do not reflect the writer's personality. • The writing lacks consistent engagement with the topic.	• The voice lacks individuality and is not concerned with or not matched to the audience. • The writing is lifeless or mechanical.
WORD CHOICE	• Words are specific, accurate and convey a precise meaning.	• Words are adequate and mostly correct.	• Limited vocabulary and/or frequent misuse of parts of speech impair understanding.
SENTENCE FLUENCY	• Sentences vary in length and structure. • Sentence beginnings are varied.	• Sentences do not vary significantly. • Some variety of sentence beginnings is attempted.	• Repetitive sentence structure, fragments, and run-on sentences make the writing difficult to follow. • Many sentences begin the same way.
CONVENTIONS	• Spelling, capitalization, and punctuation are correct. • Grammar and usage are correct. • Paragraphing tends to be correct and reinforces the organization.	• Spelling, capitalization, and punctuation are sometimes uneven. • Grammar and usage are not always correct. • Paragraphing is attempted but is not always sound.	• Spelling, capitalization, and punctuation are frequently incorrect. • Grammar and usage mistakes distort meaning. • Paragraphing is missing, irregular, or too frequent.

*Use the Personal Narrative Rubric on the WriteSmart CD if you wish to further modify this chart.

Blues Ain't No Mockin Bird

by Toni Cade Bambara

SUMMARY:

When a reporter and cameraman begin filming her property without permission and refuse to stop, Granny becomes angry and distraught at their intrusion. With his grandchildren watching in awe, Granddaddy Cain calmly takes the camera, exposes the film, and then politely asks the men to step out of Granny's garden.

RELATED NONFICTION:

LEVEL 1

BOOK EXCERPT: "Documenting the Depression"

This book excerpt describes how Paul Taylor and Dorothea Lange recorded the misery of the Great Depression with courage and compassion. (*Readability*: Average)

EDITORIAL: "Editorial: Responsible Reporting"

The author of this editorial argues for ethical, responsible reporting and calls for an end to selling and exploiting human misery. (*Readability*: Average)

LEVEL 2

NEWSPAPER ARTICLE: "He Turned His Camera on Appalachia, and One Man Wouldn't Stand For It"

This article traces the tragic results of a real filmmaker's efforts to depict poverty in a Kentucky town. (*Readability*: Average)

WEB DOCUMENT: "NPPA Code of Ethics"

The National Press Photographers Association describes the responsibilities of photographers to their audiences and to the subjects they are investigating. (*Readability*: Challenging)

FOCUS AND MOTIVATE *p. 217*

FOR ALL STUDENTS

EXPLORE THE BIG QUESTION: *"How important is SELF-RESPECT?"*
Discuss the question with students, guiding them to explore their ideas about self-respect and what it means. Then have small groups work together to complete the **Web It** activity. Point out to students that they will revisit their ideas at the end of the selection.

INTRODUCE THE LESSON Tell students that in these selections, they will explore ideas about the relationship between the media, such as reporters, photographers, and filmmakers, and their subjects. Then call their attention to the Assessment Goals at the bottom of the page.

ASSESSMENT GOALS

LEVEL 1

- examine the historical and cultural context of a work of fiction
- use active reading strategies to comprehend text
- connect a nonfiction text to other texts
- analyze a writing prompt and plan a character study

LEVEL 2

- analyze the historical and cultural context of a work of fiction
- apply critical thinking skills to analyze text
- connect a nonfiction text to other texts
- analyze a writing prompt and plan a character study

LEVEL 1

To enhance students' understanding of how **historical and cultural context** and a **writer's background** contribute to a work of literature, discuss how these factors shape and inform previous selections they have read. Choose from selections such as "The Rights to the Streets of Memphis," "The House on Mango Street," "I Have a Dream," and "Where Have You Gone, Charming Billy?" and discuss questions such as:

- What social and cultural conditions may have influenced this work?
- What were the commonly accepted social values of the time?
- What do you know about the author's background? How do factors such as ethnicity, gender, and family shape the writer's view of the world?

LEVEL 2

If helpful, review the definitions of historical and cultural context and writer's background and discuss these ideas using selections read previously, as presented in Level 1, above. You may wish to extend the discussion using these additional questions:

- How does the author communicate his or her own personal values? Are they stated directly or indirectly?
- What is the tone of the work?
- How has the author and his or her work contributed to your understanding of the specific time and place?

ADDITIONAL TERMS FOR CRITICAL ANALYSIS

To reinforce understanding of **dialect** and **idioms,** ask students to suggest examples from other works they have read. Include these points in your discussion:

- Dialect is often used to form a narrator's or character's voice. Reading the text aloud can help the reader gain a better idea of how the author intends the dialect to sound.
- Dialect can feature nonstandard grammatical construction of sentences; these constructions can also serve to form an authentic voice.
- Readers can look for context clues to help them determine the meaning of many idioms.

ADDITIONAL RESOURCES
from McDougal Littell Literature

STUDENT'S EDITION
Literary Workshop, "History, Culture, and the Author," p. 830

Additional selection questions, p. 872

STANDARDS LESSON FILE: LITERATURE
Lesson 47: Author's Perspective, p. 447

RESOURCE MANAGER
Selection Summary, pp. 75, 76

Additional Selection Questions, p. 71

Ideas for Extension, p. 72

Reading Check, p. 81

Question Support, p. 82

Selection Test A, p. 85

Selection Test B/C, p. 87

BEST PRACTICES TOOLKIT
Author's Craft, p. D24

Blues Ain't No Mockin Bird

CLOSE READ

If you are using this selection primarily for **test preparation,** direct students to preview the multiple choice questions on page 226 and the writing prompt on page 227 to help focus their reading. Explain that this technique may be used any time they take a reading test.

Summarize, page 219

Students may suggest that the narrator and Cathy live with their Granny and, as noted in lines 10–12, the family seems to have moved often to follow work opportunities. Students should be able to support their ideas with evidence from the text.

Pause & Reflect, page 220

1. MONITOR Students should underline "aunty" in lines 30 and 49, statements that do not include asking permission, such as "We thought we'd get a shot" (lines 25–26), "We thought we'd take" (line 30), and actions such as continuing to film even after Granny has said she does mind (lines 45–46).

2. DRAW CONCLUSIONS It shows that during this time, the rights of families like the narrator's were not recognized by those who saw themselves in a position of authority. *Remediation Tip:* If students have difficulty perceiving the disrespect Granny is being shown, point out that the men do not ask for permission to film—they just tell her their intentions.

Clarify, page 221

The men say they are shooting film for the "food stamp campaign" (lines 53–54); they seem to be interested in Granny's garden as a way to show that she can provide food for her family.

✓TestSmart page 221

Answer: D, "respecting people's privacy"; *Remediation Tip:* If students have difficulty inferring the reason, point out clues such as "Takin pictures of the man in his misery about to jump" (lines 72–73) and " But savin a few" (lines 74–75) that show Granny's distaste and disdain.

Clarify, page 222

Students should mark the first choice, "to get away from people who treat them with disrespect." *Remediation Tip:* If needed, point out that in lines 90–93, the narrator gives clear examples that show how her family has been disrespected.

Compare, page 222

Students should explain that this encounter follows a pattern of disrespect that Granny has experienced again and again.

Pause & Reflect, page 223

1. DRAW CONCLUSIONS Students will likely suggest that people who "go for" the narrator's grandfather are those who feel they are superior to him and, as such, resent his noble appearance.

2. ANALYZE Students may respond that it was probably a common practice to treat families like the narrator's with little or no respect.

Draw Conclusions, page 224

Students may conclude that Granddaddy Cain shows self-respect by not arguing with the men but by demanding, without saying a word, that they give him the camera. They may underline details like "He held that one hand out all still" (line 181) and those in lines 189–190 that tell how he looks directly at the men and they avoid his eyes.

Clarify, page 224

Students should make the third choice, "He pulls it apart." *Remediation Tip:* If necessary, point out how the narrator describes her grandfather's actions by using the words "gentle" and "lifts" in lines 197–198, and that while her grandfather moves quickly, he does not act aggressively.

Pause & Reflect, page 225

DRAW CONCLUSIONS Possible response: Camera man is finally getting the message that he needs to be respectful now that his camera is in the grandfather's hands.

Big Question page 225

Students may note that Granny and Granddaddy Cain show self-respect by leaving places where they are not respected and by letting their actions show that they demand to be respected. Students should draw valid connections between the story and the ideas they listed in the web on page 217.

ASSESSMENT PRACTICE I: *p. 226*	
1. D	5. C
2. C	6. A
3. B	7. A
4. A	8. D

Point out to students that the test-taking strategies they learned as they read can be used with the following items: • Items 2 and 3: infer (page 221)

Blues Ain't No Mockin Bird

SECOND READ: CRITICAL ANALYSIS

If you are using this selection primarily for **test preparation,** direct students to preview the multiple choice questions on page 226 and the writing prompt on page 227 to help focus their reading. Explain that this technique may be used any time they take a reading test.

Analyze, page 219

Students may note that lines 10–12 suggest the family seems to have moved often to follow work opportunities; they should conclude from their first reading that the family has also moved often because of the disrespect they have encountered.

Analyze, page 220

Students should circle examples of dialect such as leaving off the final *g* in verbs, as in "makin" (line 21), and "swingin" (line 24), using double negatives as in "don't never have" (line 22) and descriptors such as "Cathy grown-up" (line 22).

Draw Conclusions, page 220

Students should mark the second choice, "is a sign of disrespect," and should explain that it shows that in this time and place, the rights of families like the narrator's were not considered by those who saw themselves in a position of authority.

Draw Conclusions, page 221

Students will likely indicate that the men are making a film for the county to show that the food stamps program is a waste; they may further conclude that the author does not have a high opinion of this purpose.

✓TestSmart page 221

Answer: C, "her focus is on . . . lack of respect"

Compare, page 222

Students should explain that this encounter follows a pattern of disrespect that Granny has experienced again and again; they should conclude that this kind of disrespect was a common part of the cultural climate during the time of the story.

Analyze, page 223

Students may suggest that "go for him" means something like "go after him and put him in his place" or "show him who is in charge." The grandfather's natural stature and demeanor seem to be unacceptable, and the desire or need to put him in his place indicates that social hierarchies, while unfair and unjust, were very clear at this time.

✓TestSmart: Vocabulary, page 223

Answer: C, "upbringing"

Analyze, page 224

Students may underline examples such as how the men smile like wolves in lines 172–174, how they whisper and seem superior and yet fearful of him in lines 183–185, and avoid his direct gaze in lines 189–190. Given the cultural climate of the time, using "please" to address one's social inferior would have been very unusual; it shows how strongly Granddaddy's presence intimidates the photographer.

Draw Conclusions, page 225

Students will likely conclude that Bambara believes that these social and cultural conditions are widespread and deeply unjust. Accept all supported responses.

Big Question page 225

Accept all supported responses; most will likely suggest that, given the repeated pattern of disrespect that the narrator's family has experienced, there was no other way that the situation could have been handled that would have allowed the family to maintain their self-respect.

ASSESSMENT PRACTICE I: *p. 226*	
1. C	5. A
2. A	6. C
3. C	7. A
4. A	8. D

Point out to students that the test-taking strategies they learned as they read can be used with the following items:
- Item 1: infer (page 221)
- Items 7 and 8: use context clues (page 223)

SHORT RESPONSE: SUMMARY Use this writing activity to determine whether students understand that historical and cultural context shape a story. Take them through the following steps:

- Have students analyze the prompt. They should notice that they that they are being asked to write a summary paragraph.

- Review historical factors as they are listed under *Academic Vocabulary*. Then have them complete the chart. Point out that if it is done correctly, the chart will contain most of the content they will need to write their response.

- Students should return to the text to locate and record details that provide evidence for their answers to the questions.

TEST-TAKER'S TOOLKIT

Questions	Evidence from the Story
When does the story take place? What was happening at that time?	The story takes place in the South during the Depression. The family moves from place to place (lines 9–12); they face discrimination and disrespect (lines 87–95); the men with cameras come to film their place without asking permission (lines 51–58)
Where is the story set?	in the Southern United States on what seems to be a rural property; back porch, screen door, meadows, woods, Granddaddy Cain hunts
What were the cultural values in that time and place?	Whites did not generally view African Americans as their equals, and, as such, were not shown respect; the men call Granny "aunty," (lines 30, 49) and think it is all right to roam her property and film her and her home without her permission; the narrator explains that people "go for" Granddaddy Cain because he has self-respect (lines 128–129).

SAMPLE SUMMARY

The short story "Blues Ain't No Mockin Bird" is shaped by the historical factors and cultural issues of its time. Set in the middle of the 20th century in the Southern United States, the story reflects the discrimination African Americans faced on a regular basis. Whites did not see African Americans as their equals, as can be seen in the way the men from the county treat Granny by calling her "aunty" and filming her property without her permission. The family moves from place to place "on account of people drivin Granny crazy" by not treating them with respect. The racism of the time is also revealed in the way that whites "go for" Granddaddy Cain, because, as the narrator explains, he carries himself with enormous self-respect and white people "just can't stand it." The story's climax, when Granddaddy Cain destroys the film, hints at cultural changes to come, when African Americans will mobilize and demand equal rights.

SETTING A PURPOSE Complete the prereading activity on page 228 and review the teaching options below. Then share with your students what their goals will be, and use these goals to set a purpose for reading. Once students are clear on that purpose, have them write a purpose statement at the top of page 229.

TEST PREPARATION Direct students to read the multiple-choice questions on page 234, as well as the writing prompt on page 235, to help them focus their reading.

<table>
<tr><td>

LEVEL 1

</td><td>

LEVEL 2

</td></tr>
<tr><td>

• Documenting the Depression
• Editorial: Responsible Reporting

FOCUS SKILL: CONNECT TEXTS

ACTIVITY: ANTICIPATION/REACTION GUIDE

Have partners complete the left column of the chart before you assign the readin. Have them complete the right column of the chart after reading.

OPTIONS FOR TEACHING

SKILL INSTRUCTION Use "Learn the Skill" at the bottom of page 228 and page R2 in the Nonfiction Skills Handbook to review the focus skill of connecting texts.

> **ADDITIONAL RESOURCES:**
> **STANDARDS LESSON FILE:** READING AND INFORMATIONAL TEXTS: Lesson 11: Compare Treatment, Organization, and Scope, page 265

DISCUSSION Divide the class into small groups, each responsible for learning and then sharing information about one of the following questions:
- Do journalists have a right and a responsibility to report whatever they feel is newsworthy?
- Can an image really bring change to the world?
- Which idea from the nonfiction selections do you find most controversial? Why?
- In what ways has the Internet affected journalism?

If you are using Level 2 in the same classroom, have mixed groups briefly describe and summarize the texts they have read before they begin their discussion.

INVESTIGATION Have partners investigate journalists such as Dorothea Lange, Mathew Brady, Jacob Riis, and Margaret Bourke-White. Have students share examples of each journalist's work with the class.

</td><td>

• He Turned His Camera on Appalachia, and One Man Wouldn't Stand For It
• NPPA Code of Ethics

FOCUS SKILL: CONNECT TEXTS

ACTIVITY: LIST IT

Before assigning the related readings, have students fill out the chart and discuss their ideas in small groups.

OPTIONS FOR TEACHING

SKILL INSTRUCTION Use "Learn the Skill" at the bottom of page 228 and page R2 in the Nonfiction Skills Handbook to review the focus skill of connecting texts.

> **ADDITIONAL RESOURCES:**
> **STANDARDS LESSON FILE:** READING AND INFORMATIONAL TEXTS: Lesson 11: Compare Treatment, Organization, and Scope, page 265

FILM SCREENING Arrange for students to see all or parts of "Stranger With a Camera." Then ask students:
- Which elements of the film affected you most?
- How are the ideas in the film related to the selections you have read?
- How is seeing a film about the event different from reading about it?

If you are using Level 1 in the same classroom, ask students to compare the ideas about journalism in the selections they have read with those in the film.

CREATE A JOURNALISM BANK Have groups compile a list of news sources they turn to when they want to learn about an important news event, and discuss why they find these sources to be responsible.

</td></tr>
</table>

Documenting the Depression

Connect Texts, page 229
Students should mark stars and make notes throughout in the margins that show they are connecting ideas between texts. They may note historical connections, how times are documented, and connections between characters such as Granddaddy Cain, Granny, and the migrant mother.

Specialized Vocabulary, page 230
The migrants moved from place to place to find work harvesting crops.

Monitor, page 230
Students should box lines 43–45, "The mother received food . . . quickly printed the image."

Make Judgments, page 231
Accept reasonable responses; students should clearly note the power of the image, its subject, and its meanings.

Connect Texts, page 231
Possible response for first sentence: have to move constantly to find work to support their families. Possible response for second sentence: respected her subjects and used her work to improve their lives.

Editorial: Responsible Reporting

Connect Texts, page 232
Students' marks and notes in the margins should reflect active thinking about connections between the three texts.

✓TestSmart page 232
Answer: B, "sell magazines and newspapers"; *Remediation Tip*: If students mark another choice, have them return to lines 51–68 and summarize the main point of the editorial.

Specialized Vocabulary, page 233
Students should indicate that they understand that businesses seek to make profit; they should underline this idea in lines 71–76.

Connect Texts, page 233
Students should explain that Dorothea Lange adhered closely to the ideas in *Guidelines for Responsible Reporting,* while the photographer in "Blues Ain't No Mockin Bird" seemed to have little regard for truth, integrity, and respect.

ASSESSMENT PRACTICE II: *p. 234*	
1. A	5. D
2. A	6. D
3. C	7. C
4. C	8. B

He Turned His Camera on Appalachia, and One Man Wouldn't Stand For It

Connect Texts, page 229
Students' marks and notes throughout the margins should show they can connect ideas between texts. They may note historical connections, how times are documented, and connections between characters such as Granddaddy Cain, Granny, and the individuals in the article.

Specialized Vocabulary, page 229
If necessary, point out that while documentary makers see their work as nonfiction, they sometimes have predetermined ideas and opinions about their subjects.

Make Judgments, page 230
Students should underline the sentence "It seemed ennobling . . ." (lines 77–80), ideas in lines 84–90, those about President Johnson's War on Poverty in lines 91–100. They may double-underline "feeling embarrassed" (line 103), and "being snooped on" (line 118). Accept any reasonable, supported ideas about which view seems most valid.

Connect Texts, page 231
Possible response for first statement: two people felt their lives were being intruded upon disrespectfully. Possible response for second statement: acted cruelly and violently.

NPPA Code of Ethics

Connect Texts, page 232
Students' marks and notes in the margins should reflect active thinking about connections between the three texts.

Summarize, page 232
The NPPA thinks the role of photojournalists is to be responsible reporters of significant events and ideas.
Remediation Tip: If students have difficulty in their response, point out the explicit roles the NPPA outlines in lines 8–13.

Make Judgments, page 233
Accept all reasonable, supported opinions. Some responses might indicate that it is not "always" possible to respect privacy.

Connect Texts, page 233
Accept all reasonable, supported opinions; students should clearly explain their ideas. Examples of how the men in the story did not follow the code of ethics might include the fact that they did not treat Granny with respect and dignity when they called her "aunty" and when they filmed without her permission, that they had a political involvement by working "for the county," and that they were not unobtrusive and humble.

ASSESSMENT PRACTICE II: *p. 234*	
1. D	5. B
2. A	6. D
3. C	7. B
4. C	8. D

LEVEL 1

Guide students through the steps described below under Guided Instruction. You may also wish to go over the rubric on the next page. (Consider modifying the rubric for these students, focusing only on Ideas, Organization, and Conventions.) Give students the entire 30 minutes to draft and review their responses. Point out, however, that in an actual timed writing situation, all steps of the writing process must be completed within the given time frame.

LEVEL 2

Share with students the rubric on the next page. Direct them to complete the entire writing process independently, within the actual 30-minute time frame they have been given.

GUIDED INSTRUCTION

ANALYZE THE PROMPT If necessary, lead students through the two-step analysis process on page 235. Explain that low scores are often the result of the writer missing a critical piece of the directions. The marked prompt should look like this:

> How would you describe Granny's character in the short story "Blues Ain't No Mockin Bird"? Identify and discuss two of Granny's character traits in a three- to five-paragraph response. Be sure to use descriptive language that conveys Granny's personality. Include evidence from the story to support your character study.

- *Academic Vocabulary*: Explain that a **character study** discusses a single character's unique traits and personality. Point out that in this prompt, two traits must be discussed.

- Remind students that all the elements they circled in the prompt have to be addressed in their responses if they want to achieve the highest score on the test.

PLAN YOUR RESPONSE

- Review with students the steps of a timed writing assignment. For a prompt like this, which requires them to find and include evidence, remind them to budget enough time to find evidence. (They should probably spend no more than 5–10 minutes identifying their examples.)

- Students should use the chart to jot down notes about Granny's traits and evidence from the story. Point out, however, that in a real testing situation, they would have had to identify two traits themselves and supply the examples.

WRITE AND REVIEW Encourage students to choose the best evidence from the text and use it in a creative way (using peer feedback to choose the most effective if time allows). Remind them that the prompt directs them to use descriptive language to describe Granny. When they have completed their draft, allow peers to comment on how well the students have met the requirements of the prompt.

RUBRIC FOR TIMED WRITING*

KEY TRAITS	3 (STRONG)	2 (AVERAGE)	1 (WEAK)
IDEAS	• The character is identified and the main impression or focus of the character study is clearly conveyed. • The key character traits are well explained by relevant details and examples.	• The character is identified, but the main impression or focus of the character study is vague. • Most details and examples are relevant in explaining key character traits.	• No main impression of the character is identified. • Details and examples are irrelevant or missing and do not explain key character traits.
ORGANIZATION	• The introduction clearly presents the character and engages the reader. • The conclusion summarizes the ideas and draws a conclusion or offers an observation. • The writer chooses clear and suitable transition words. • The organization is logical and follows a consistent pattern.	• The introduction presents an identifiable character but does not draw the reader in. • The conclusion summarizes the ideas but only restates what has been said. • The writer uses some transitions, but a few more are needed. • The organization may have occasional inconsistencies.	• The introduction does not clearly identify the subject of the study. • The study lacks an identifiable conclusion. • The writer uses few, if any, transitional words. • The organization feels random or disjointed; the reader often feels lost or confused.
VOICE	• The tone and voice are appropriate for the purpose and audience. • The writing reflects active engagement with the character.	• The tone and voice are acceptable but not strongly individual or direct. • The writing lacks consistent engagement with the character.	• The voice lacks individuality and is not concerned with or not matched to the audience. • The writing is lifeless or mechanical.
WORD CHOICE	• Words and phrases precisely describe the character's appearance, actions, speech, personality, and other traits.	• Words and phrases generally describe the character's appearance, actions, speech, personality, and other traits.	• Limited vocabulary and/or frequent misuse of parts of speech impair understanding.
SENTENCE FLUENCY	• Sentences vary in length and structure. • Sentence beginnings are varied.	• Sentences do not vary significantly. • Sentence beginnings are mostly the same.	• Sentence structure makes the writing hard to follow. • Most or all sentences begin the same way.
CONVENTIONS	• Spelling, capitalization, and punctuation are correct. • Grammar and usage are correct. • Paragraphing tends to be correct and reinforces the organization.	• Spelling, capitalization, and punctuation are sometimes uneven. • Grammar and usage are not always correct. • Paragraphing is attempted but is not always sound.	• Spelling, capitalization, and punctuation are frequently incorrect. • Grammar and usage mistakes distort meaning. • Paragraphing is missing, irregular, or too frequent.

*Use the Character Sketch Rubric on the WriteSmart CD if you wish to further modify this chart.

Diagnostic Assessments

Student Self-Assessment: Reading

Directions: Use this form to describe your attitude and thoughts toward reading at this time. You may circle more than one answer on any item.

1. These are my thoughts and attitude about reading:

   a. I like to read, both at home and at school.
   b. I like to read for fun, but not for school.
   c. I really don't like to read and would rather do other things.
   d. I would read more if I were a better reader.
   e. I would like to read if I had more time.

2. These are my thoughts and attitude about reading at home:

   a. It's a waste of time.
   b. It helps me escape and relax.
   c. I only read when I have to for an assignment.
   d. I read mostly for entertainment.
   e. I read mostly for information.
   f. I love to read and wish I had more time for it.

3. I consider myself to be

   a. a very good reader.
   b. a good reader.
   c. an average reader.
   d. a poor reader.

4. In order to read and understand material for school,

   a. I read best when I'm alone in a quiet place.
   b. I read best with things going on around me.
   c. I read best around with another student or in a small group.
   d. I read best when the teacher tells us what to look for first.
   e. I understand more when I have a long period of time to read.
   f. I understand more when I read in short little spurts.
   g. I read the material twice.

5. These problems bother me when I am reading:

   a. There are too many words that I don't know.
   b. I read too slowly.
   c. I read too fast and forget things.
   d. I get bored quickly and stop paying attention.
   e. My eyes get tired easily.
   f. Other things distract me.

6. How often do you read each of the following? Circle your answer.

a. newspapers	never	sometimes	often	usually
b. magazines	never	sometimes	often	usually
c. novels	never	sometimes	often	usually
d. comic books	never	sometimes	often	usually
e. books of information	never	sometimes	often	usually

7. How much time do you spend at home reading for enjoyment?

   a. never

   b. up to 30 minutes a week

   c. between 30 and 60 minutes a week

   d. more than an hour a week

   e. an hour a day or more

8. Circle the topics or types of literature you like to read.

a. young adult novels	**i.** fantasy
b. adventure/survival	**j.** myths and legends
c. science fiction	**k.** science
d. mysteries	**l.** poetry
e. sports	**m.** biographies
f. stories about animals	**n.** history
g. humorous stories	**o.** travel/other places
h. historical fiction	**p.** news articles

9. What is the best book you have ever read?

   _____

10. What is the best book you have read lately?

    _____

11. Look at the scale below and put an X where you think you belong.

    I am not good at reading.   I am OK at reading.   I am good at reading.

    _____

    1   2   3   4   5   6   7   8   9   10

Informal Reading Inventory

This informal inventory can give an initial idea of a student's reading level. Teachers often use an Informal Reading Inventory (IRI) to place students in the appropriate textbook or to help them find books or articles for independent reading.

To conduct an IRI, you need at least one 100-word passage from the material in question, and 10 comprehension questions about the material. Have the student read the same passage twice; the first time orally to assess oral reading skills. The student should read the passage a second time silently, after which he or she answers questions for assessment of reading comprehension. Use these suggestions to administer this IRI.

1. Tell the student he or she will read the passage out loud, and then again silently, and then you will ask some questions.

2. Give the students a copy of the passage and keep one for yourself. Have the student read the passage. As students read aloud, note on your copy the number of errors he or she makes.

   - *Mispronunciations:* Words that are mispronounced, with the exception of proper nouns.
   - *Omissions:* Words left out that are crucial to understanding a sentence or a concept.
   - *Additions:* Words inserted in a sentence that change the meaning of the text.
   - *Substitutions:* Words substituted for actual words in the text that change the meaning of a sentence. (An acceptable substitution might be the word *hard* for the word *difficult.*)

   Use these criteria for assessing reading levels after oral reading:

   - *Fewer than 3 errors:* The student is unlikely to have difficulty decoding text.
   - *Between 4 and 9 errors:* The student is likely to have some difficulty, may need special attention.
   - *More than 10 errors:* The student is likely to have great difficulty, may need placement in a less demanding reading program.

3. Have the student read the passage again, silently.

4. When the student finishes, ask the comprehension questions on the next page. Tell the students that he or she can look back at the passage before answering the questions.

5. Note the number of correct responses. Use these criteria for assessing reading level after silent reading.

   - *Eight or more:* The student should be able to interpret the selections effectively.
   - *Five to seven:* The student is likely to have difficulty.
   - *Fewer than five:* The student needs individual help or alternate placement.

6. Evaluate results from oral and silent reading to decide how good a match the material is for a student.

from "Marigolds"
by Eugenia Collier

By the time I was 14 my brother Joey and I were the only children left at our house, the older ones having left home for early marriage or the lure of the city, and the two babies having been sent to relatives who might care for them better than we. Joey was three years younger than I, and a boy, and therefore vastly inferior. Each morning our mother and father trudged wearily down the dirt road and around the bend, she to her domestic job and he to his daily unsuccessful quest for work. After our few chores around the tumbledown shanty, Joey and I were free to run wild in the sun with other children similarly situated.

---

number of mispronunciations: _____

number of omissions: _____

number of additions: _____

number of substitutions: _____

Total: _____

Comprehension Questions

from "Marigolds
by Eugenia Collier

1. How old is the narrator?

_____

2. What is her brother's name?

_____

3. How old is the narrator's brother?

_____

4. How do you know the narrator is a girl?

_____

5. Why did her older siblings leave home?

_____

6. Where have the two babies been sent?

_____

7. Where does her mother go each morning?

_____

8. Where does her father go?

_____

9. What do the narrator and her brother do when their parents leave?

_____

10. How does she describe her home?

_____

Number of correct answers: _____

Administering a Cloze Test

Another test that has proven successful in determining reading skill levels is the cloze test. Cloze is a psychological term which refers to the human tendency to "bring to closure" a familiar but incomplete pattern. The test is based on "filling in" blanks created in a passage of text unfamiliar to students. The cloze procedure is often used to place students in informational texts, but can also be used in other reading situations, where you want to match a student's reading level with materials. A cloze test is created in the following way:

- Select a passage of 250–300 words that contains a complete thought unit or several paragraphs, preferably from the beginning of the article or book.
- Delete every 5th word in the passage, excluding the opening sentence.
- Leave a blank for each word deleted. You should have approximately 50 blanks.
- For each blank, have students generate the exact word that has been deleted.

Use these suggestions to administer this cloze test.

1. Give the students a copy of the passage.
2. Tell them to read the passage and to fill in the blanks with the words that have been deleted from the passage.
3. Use the following to determine reading level. This particular passage has 48 blanks.
   - independent level: 58% correct answers or more, or 28 of 48
   - instructional level: 44–57% correct answers, or 21–27 of 48
   - frustration level: 43% correct answers or less or fewer than 21 of 48

Some researchers have modified the cloze procedure as developed by John Bormuth. For example, some have suggested replacing significant words or every 10th word, and accepting synonyms; however, the scoring system above applies only when the process described above is used.

For the complete passage, see the next page.

Cloze Test: Answer

Every night after dinner, my mother and I would sit at the Formica kitchen table. She would present new <u>tests</u>, taking her examples from <u>stories</u> of amazing children she <u>had</u> read in *Ripley's Believe* <u>*It*</u> *or Not,* or *Good* <u>*Housekeeping*</u>*, Reader's Digest,* and a <u>dozen</u> other magazines she kept <u>in</u> a pile in our <u>bathroom</u>. My mother got these <u>magazines</u> from people whose houses <u>she</u> cleaned. And since she <u>cleaned</u> many houses each week, <u>we</u> had a great assortment. <u>She</u> would look through them <u>all</u>, searching for stories about <u>remarkable</u> children.

The first night <u>she</u> brought out a story <u>about</u> a three-year-old boy who <u>knew</u> the capitals of all <u>the</u> states and even most of the European countries. A <u>teacher</u> was quoted as saying <u>the</u> little boy could also <u>pronounce</u> the names of the <u>foreign</u> cities correctly.

"What's the <u>capital</u> of Finland?" my mother <u>asked</u> me, looking at the <u>magazine</u> story. All I knew <u>was</u> the capital of California, <u>because</u> Sacramento was the name <u>of</u> the street we lived <u>on</u> in Chinatown. "Nairobi!" I <u>guessed</u>, saying the most foreign <u>word</u> I could think of. She <u>checked</u> to see if <u>that</u> was possibly one way <u>to</u> pronounce "Helsinki" before showing <u>me</u> the answer.

The tests <u>got</u> harder —multiplying numbers in <u>my</u> head, finding the queen <u>of</u> hearts in a deck <u>of</u> cards, trying to stand <u>on</u> my head without using <u>my</u> hands, predicting the daily <u>temperatures</u> in Los Angeles, New <u>York</u>, and London

from "Two Kinds"
by Amy Tan

Read the passage below. On a separate sheet of paper, fill in the blanks with the words that have been deleted from the passage.

Every night after dinner, my mother and I would sit at the Formica kitchen table. She would present new [1], taking her examples from[2] of amazing children she[3] read in Ripley's Believe [4] or Not, or Good [5], Reader's Digest, and a[6] other magazines she kept [7] a pile in our [8]. My mother got these[9] from people whose houses[10] cleaned. And since she[11] many houses each week, [12] had a great assortment.[13] would look through them[14], searching for stories about[15] children.

The first night[16] brought out a story[17] a three-year-old boy who [18]the capitals of all [19] states and even most [20] the European countries. A [21] was quoted as saying [22] little boy could also [23] the names of the[24] cities correctly.

"What's the [25] of Finland?" my mother [26] me, looking at the [27] story. All I knew[28] the capital of California,[29] Sacramento was the name [30] the street we lived [31] in Chinatown. "Nairobi!" I [32], saying the most foreign [33] I could think of. [34] checked to see if [35] was possibly one way [36] pronounce "Helsinki" before showing [37] the answer.

The tests[38] harder—multiplying numbers in [39] head, finding the queen [40] hearts in a deck [41] cards, trying to stand[42] my head without using [43] hands, predicting the daily[44] in Los Angeles, New [45], and London.

Number of blanks: 45
Number of correct insertions: _____
% correct: _____